Lydia Liakhovskaya

RUSSIAN CUISINE

Text by
LYDIA LIAKHOVSKAYA

Translated from the Russian by
VALERY FATEYEV

Designed by
NIKOLAI KUTOVOI

Illustrations by
ANTON LOMAYEV
and ALEXEI ORLEANSKY

Computer type-setting by
YELENA MOROZOVA and
ALEXANDER SHCHEGLOV

Colour proofs
by LIUBOV KORNEYEVA
and VLADIMIR GLAZKOV

Photographs by
GEORGY KHORDAS,
ARTHUR KIRAKOZOV,
LYDIA LIAKHOVSKAYA,
VLADIMIR MELNIKOV,
VICTOR POLIAKOV,
YEKATERINA
POSETSELSKAYA,
VICTOR SAVIK,
VLADIMIR VDOVIN,
VASILY VORONTSOV
and VICTOR YEREMEYEV

Editor-in-Chief:
SERGEI VESNIN

Managing editor:
MARIA LYZHENKOVA

ISBN 5-8194-0010-0

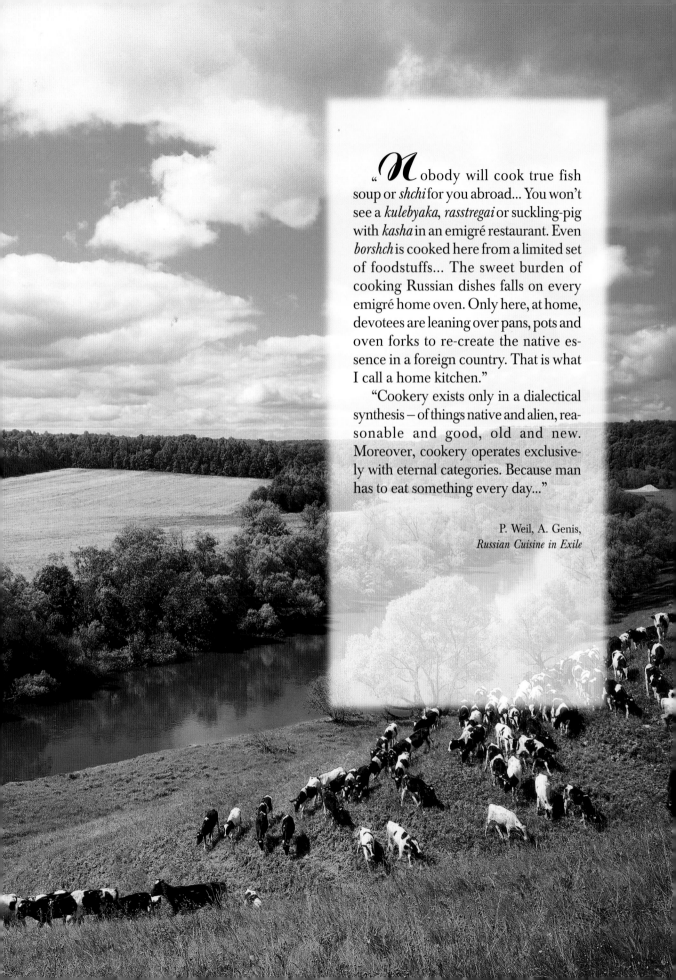

„**N**obody will cook true fish soup or *shchi* for you abroad... You won't see a *kulebyaka*, *rasstregai* or suckling-pig with *kasha* in an emigré restaurant. Even *borshch* is cooked here from a limited set of foodstuffs... The sweet burden of cooking Russian dishes falls on every emigré home oven. Only here, at home, devotees are leaning over pans, pots and oven forks to re-create the native essence in a foreign country. That is what I call a home kitchen."

"Cookery exists only in a dialectical synthesis – of things native and alien, reasonable and good, old and new. Moreover, cookery operates exclusively with eternal categories. Because man has to eat something every day..."

P. Weil, A. Genis,
Russian Cuisine in Exile

CONTENTS

ZAKUSKAS OR HORS-D'OEUVRES SALADS

A zakuska or hors-d'oeuvre is a salted or piquant appetizer supposed to be eaten before a meal. Therefore it is as an overture to a festive dinner.

It was in Russia, as some sources suggest, that the tradition to serve *zakuskas* at the beginning of a meal emerged. The very conditions of Russian life predetermined such a culinary tradition, because the austere Russian climate taught people to have good supplies of various foodstuffs at home throughout the long winter. And therefore salted, cured and smoked fish, meat, game and poultry, as well as salted and pickled vegetables and mushrooms, mostly home-made, were stored in abundance. That is why *zakuskas,* an indispensable feature of the Russian cuisine, are so diverse. In addition to distinctly national specialties such as caviar, salted, jerked and smoked or dried dishes, present-day *zakuskas* in a general sense have included West European patés, meat-jellies, sandwiches, salads and seafood.

7

Salted Salmon

Prepare salmon by removing small bones out of the fillet. Sprinkle it with a coarse-ground salt and let it stay at room temperature for two days in summer and three days in winter, after which the fish is ready.

Salted Herring

Salted herring is the best hors-d'oeuvre to be served with Russian vodka. It is usually preferred as a cold dish both for an everyday meal and for a festive dinner.

Take care to choose a herring of silver-grey sheen with bright, succulent and soft meat.

Hot-Smoked Sturgeon

Salt chunks of sturgeon and leave them for an hour. Roll in a gauze, bind up and smoke for no less than 3 hours. Carve the chunks into serving-size portions, decorate with green parsley, lettuce leaves, slices of lemon and serve with vodka or white wine.

Cut the fillet diagonally, put it into a herring-dish and embellish with an onion bulb shaped as a flower and tinted by a beet juice. The combination of silvery-grey and pale yellow tints will gladden the eye and the dish itself will meet the discriminating taste of a true connoisseur of strong drinks and appropriate hors-d'oeuvres.

Crayfish with Beer

Crayfish are a very suitable accompaniment to such a popular drink as beer.

It is believed that crayfish are especially delicious between May and September. Drop washed living crayfish into salted boiling water and add a large amount of dill, parsley, tarragon, bay leaf, fragrant pepper, onion and carrot. Bring to the boiling point and cook covered for 10 to 12 minutes. Boiled crayfish have red tests, and this is an evidence of readiness. Crayfish can be served both hot and cold. Crayfish necks are a well-known delicacy. Remove ready crayfish from heat and let cool for 10 to 15 minutes in their concoction so that they acquire a particularly pleasant fragrance.

Fried Mussels

For 1 serving: 100 g (3½ oz) mussels, 1 onion, vegetable oil, a dint each of salt and sugar
For the pink sauce: 2 tbsp. mayonnaise, 1 tsp. sour cream, 1 tsp. tomato paste, 1 clove garlic

Cut onion into four parts, add a dint of sugar and sauté lightly in a pan until golden. Add prepared mussels and fry with the onion.

Garnish with olives, slices of lemon and curly parsley.

Serve with pink sauce for beer or white wine.

Smoked White Fish

True masters in the world of culinary art can give a great delight to their clients. In the Podvoriye Restaurant, you will savour an exquisite delicacy – smoked white fish – cooked by such masters according to their own recipes.

"Caviar in boat-shaped crystal bowls, cooled in ice, white fish in parsley, all sorts of salmon, mounds of pressed caviar, mounds of cheese, a sturgeon gristle in vinegar..." – this mouth-watering description by Ivan Shmelev, an emigré writer, gives some idea of the plentiful Moscow table on a festive day in pre-revolutionary Russia. Caviar features prominently in this recollection and it really occupies a pride of place in the Russian cuisine.

In numerous taverns on the Volga, for example, they used to disembowel a just caught and still alive sturgeon in the presence of a guest, to season caviar with salt and to invite the guest to taste it right away. They used to eat caviar by tablespoons drinking vodka after that.

Caviar served with *blinis*, eggs stuffed with caviar, caviar with finely minced onions and caviar served in large special bowls – all this was a common thing in Russia. Caviar was eaten with tablespoons and accompanied by hot *blinis*, icy champagne, chilled transparent vodka or strong hot and sweet tea.

Russian caviar was and has still remained the choicest delicacy and the best dish to treat a guest. The most tasty are unpressed black sturgeon caviar and the red caviar of the Far East salmon variety.

Fish Assortment

For 1 serving: 50 g (1¾ oz) each of salted and buttered salmon, hot-smoked sturgeon with lemon, boiled sturgeon with horse-radish and cold-smoked sturgeon, 30 g (1 oz) each red and black caviar, greens, olives

An assorted fish ranks with the most relished delicacies among a great variety of *zakuskas* offered by the Russian cuisine. Choose for the assortment differently coloured products which allow you to create a picturesque display. Place on a serving dish with lettuce leaves boiled sturgeon cut in slices and rolled in the shape of roses, as well as cold-smoked sturgeon, pieces of hot-smoked sturgeon, slices of Siberian salmon, red and black caviar in rose-shaped egg "baskets". Garnish the assortment with lemon, green lettuce, parsley sprigs and olives; serve sauce and horse-radish. Russian vodka and white wine are the best drinks helping one appreciate the rare delicacy of the fish assortment.

Pickled Lampreys

For the pickle: 4 parts of 9% vinegar to 7 parts of water; salt, sugar, black pepper and sweet peas to taste; cloves, bay leaf

The culinary processing of a lamprey involves just a removal of its head and mucus which is sometimes poisonous. To do this, grasp the lamprey by the head with your left hand and taking a handful of salt in your right hand, rub the fish all over removing the mucus and salting the lamprey at the same time. Cut off the head. Let the fish stay for 30 to 60 minutes and then, after washing and drying, it is prepared for frying, baking, pickling or smoking.

For pickling, brown lampreys lightly on both sides and then cook them until ready in the oven. After chilling, put them into a porcelain vessel, pour over cooled marinade and keep for 3 to 4 days in a cold light-protected room or in a refrigerator. For the marinade, mix water with vinegar in due proportion, add condiments and spices, bring to a boil, remove from the heat, cool and pour it over the lampreys.

Boiled Sturgeon with Horse-Radish

Pour cold water over prepared sturgeon, bring to a boil and skim off the foam. Add sliced salted cucumber and cucumber brine, and simmer the sturgeon covered until ready. Such method of cooking is preferable to attain the best appearance and taste of the sturgeon. Carve the chilled sturgeon with a thin knife into slices ¼-inch thick and decorate them with olives, lemon slices, green parsley, lettuce leaves and a tomato shaped as a flower. Best served with horse-radish and white wine.

Assorted Seafood

Put prepared, boiled and sautéed seafood – crabs, crayfish, mussels, squids and scallops – on a serving dish arranging them in the form of bouquets, and decorate the assortment with fresh cucumbers, tomatoes, a lace of thinly sliced sweet red pepper, lettuce and parsley.

To make the pink sauce served with seafood, you need: 2 tbsp. mayonnaise, 1 tsp. sour cream, 1 clove minced garlic and 1 tsp. tomato juice.

Liver Paté

650 g (1 lb 7 oz) liver, ½ cup butter or poultry fat, 150 g (5 oz) lard, 1 small onion, 1 carrot, 2 or 3 tbsp.
milk or broth, salt and ground black pepper to taste, greens

Sauté chopped carrots and onions with lard until half-ready, then add diced liver. Season with salt and pepper and fry until done. Chill. Put through a mincer twice. Add fat, milk or broth and mix until well blended. Shape into a loaf and cut. Garnish with fresh cucumbers, tomatoes or canned fruit.

Boiled Tongue with Horse-Radish

For 1 serving: 100 g (3½ oz) tongue

Immerse beef or calf tongue in cold water, add salt, spices and aromatic roots. Boil for 2 to 3 hours. Immediately peel the boiled tongue after slightly cooling it under running water. Dip into the concoction again, bring to a boil, cool in the concoction and cut into slices. Garnish with green pies, fresh cucumbers, tomatoes and herbs. Serve with horse-radish.

Sandwich Hors-d'oeuvre Cake

Round loaf of rye bread, 2 tbsp. butter, 3 lemon slices, 12 to 15 sprats, 5 leaves of green onions, 5 to 7 strips of red sweet fresh or canned pepper, 1 boiled carrot, several cloves garlic

Cut off the upper part of a rye bread loaf. Cut the rest of the round loaf into two layers, butter the lower one, put the upper layer on top and butter it too. Arrange in a fan-like fashion sprats, green onions, pieces of sweet red pepper, cloves of garlic and lemon slices, and adorn the serving dish with a flower made of carrot.

Chicken under Walnut Sauce

For 2 servings: 1 chicken
For the sauce: 300 g (10 oz) onion, 2 cups chopped walnuts, 2 tbsp. wheat flour, ½ cup butter, 2 egg yolks, salt, lemon juice, ground red, black and fragrant pepper, cloves, nutmeg and coriander, greens

Boil a chicken and cool it, bone the meat and strain the broth. To prepare sauce in the Podvoriye Restaurant style, put onion through a mincer, pour in boiling water so that it just covers the onion and place on a heat stirring occasionally until the liquid evaporates. Then add chicken fat and butter, sauté onions, make a roux of flour in butter and add it, pour in chicken broth and bring the sauce to the consistency of thick sour cream. Add to the sauce chopped walnuts and garlic and egg yolks. Mix the ingredients and add salt, lemon juice and spices to taste.

Cut up the cooked chicken, lay the pieces on a serving dish, pour walnut sauce over them and decorate the dish with walnut kernels, green parsley, coriander and lettuce leaves.

Mushrooms in Sour Cream

300 g (10 oz) field mushrooms, 1 tbsp. flour, 2 tbsp. butter, 1 onion, 1 cup sour cream, salt, green parsley

Cut fresh field mushrooms in narrow strips, sauté them, add sliced onion and fry lightly with mushrooms until golden. Immerse the mushrooms into sour cream sauce, sprinkle with melted butter and serve at once, after having decorated the serving dish with small uncut mushrooms and green parsley.

To cook the sauce, make a roux of flour in two tablespoons of butter, pour in sour cream, bring to a boil and salt.

Salad of Prunes with Walnut Fillings

2¼ cups prunes, 2 cups walnuts, 3 or 4 cloves garlic, 1½ cups sour cream, 2 tsp. sugar, a squeeze of 1 lemon, salt

Pour cold boiled water over prunes so that it just covers the berries. Put the soaked and pitted berries on a culinary board to make them dry. Pound walnuts and garlic in a mortar until well blended into a uniform oily mixture, add salt and lemon juice and grind the mixture until white. Fill each berry with walnut meat, put the berries into a salad-bowl, pour in sour cream mixed with sugar and adorn the salad with walnut kernels and slices of lemon.

Beetroot Salad with Prunes and Apples

1 beetroot, 2 apples, a squeeze of half a lemon, a handful each of prunes and walnuts, 2 cloves garlic, ½ cup mayonnaise, salt, sugar, greens

Boil beetroot, or better bake it in the oven, cool in cold water, pare and grate. Grate apples too and sprinkle them with lemon juice. Mince garlic and a part of walnuts; cut prunes, which have previously been soaked in cold boiled water, into pieces. Combine all the ingredients, add salt, sugar and sour cream mixed with mayonnaise, stir and put the mixture into a salad-bowl, over lettuce leaves. Decorate the salad with walnuts and sprigs of parsley.

Tomatoes Stuffed with Meat Salad

1 kg (2 lb 3 oz) smooth and attractive tomatoes, 100 g (3½ oz) meat, 100 g (3½ oz) potatoes, 100 g (3½) oz fresh cucumbers, 1 egg, 2 tbsp. mayonnaise, salt, ground black pepper, lettuce leaves, green dill, celery and parsley

Dice boiled potatoes, egg, meat and fresh cucumber, add salt, pepper and mayonnaise mixed with finely chopped dill. Use the salad for filling tomatoes. For this purpose, cut about a quarter off each tomato, remove some pulp making a depression, add a little salt and pepper. Fill the tomatoes with the salad, place them on a serving dish over lettuce leaves and add herbs.

Cucumbers may be stuffed with a salad of fish, mushrooms or chopped eggs combined with herring as well as with various fillings based on cheese or herring oil.

Salad:
The Speckled Hen

For 1 serving: 75 g (2½ oz) chicken meat, 1 fresh cucumber, 1 egg, a handful each of prunes and walnuts, 3 to 4 tbsp. mayonnaise, green dill, parsley and lettuce leaves

Boil chicken until ready, take off meat from bones, let it get cold and cut the meat into thin narrow strips. Put lettuce leaves into a salad-bowl and spread over them slices of fresh cucumbers cut in strips and the chicken meat, scatter minced prunes, pour over mayonnaise, sprinkle chopped walnuts and greens, and decorate with sections of egg, prunes and whole walnut kernels.

Radish Salad with Cracklings

250 g (8 oz) black radish, 50 g (1¾ oz) goose cracklings with fat, salt

Grate peeled radish so that you have thin shavings. Dice goose fat and sauté it thoroughly on a pan, until the cracklings brown. Salt the radish, pour the hot goose fat over it, stir and sprinkle with cracklings.

ZAKUSKA PIES
AND PASTIES

*V*arious pies, *rasstegais, kulebyakas* and all kinds of small pasties are the Russians' favourites both during holidays and in every-day life, as well as an indispensable hors-d'oeuvre to accompany fish soup or *shchi.*

Moscow Rasstegai with Mushrooms and Rice (old recipe)

Yeast dough: 1 kg (2 lb 3 oz)
For the filling: 100 g (3½ oz) dried mush-rooms, 1 onion, 2 or 3 tbsp. butter, ½ cup rice, salt, ground black pepper
For the greasing: 1 egg yolk or 1 tbsp. butter

Boil and strain mushrooms (reserving the broth), wash them, squeeze the liquid, chop and sauté in butter. Combine the mushrooms with slightly browned onion and boiled crumbly rice, and season with butter, salt and pepper. If the filling is too dry, add some mushroom broth or a tablespoon of butter.

Roll the dough into a round flat cake, lay it on a pan, spread the prepared filling on the dough in a smooth layer and fold the edges of the dough over so that they are ¾-inch higher than the filling, leav-ing the centre of the *rasstegai* open. Brush the edges with yolk or butter. To make the pie more inviting, you can adorn it with small mushrooms, leaves and sprigs modelled of the dough and also greased. Bake the *rasstegai* at 356° to 392° F.

27

Kurnik (Chicken Pie)

Kurniks or chicken pies were traditionally baked on festive days. They were highlights at the royal table on solemn occasions as early as the reign of Ivan the Terrible. The tradition to cook *kurniks* survives to the present day, and in many regions of Russia there is a custom to bake this kind of pie for a wedding feast. Traditionally, chicken pies were baked in the homes of both the bridegroom and the bride. The bridegroom's pie used to be decorated with human figurines which implied the stability of the future family, and the bride's pie was embellished with flowers as symbols of beauty and tenderness.

Kurniks were usually filled with chicken meat, boletus mushrooms, rice, hard-boiled eggs and greens.

For the unleavened dough: 2 cups wheat flour, ½ cup butter, 1 tbsp. sugar, 1 egg, 1/3 cup milk or cream, 1 tbsp. sour cream, a dint of salt and soda
For the filling: 1 chicken, 300 g (10 oz)
fresh boletus mushrooms, 5 hard-boiled eggs, 1 cup rice, 1 tbsp. minced green parsley
For the sauce: 2 tbsp. butter, 1 tbsp. flour, 2 cups strong chicken broth, ½ cup cream, 2 egg yolks
For the greasing: 2 egg yolks

Melt butter, add cream, sour cream, egg, salt and sugar. Stir up thoroughly. Put in flour mixed with soda and knead a dough of consistently uniform quality. Unleavened dough is easier to prepare, it readily takes and keeps form. All decorations moulded with the use of this kind of dough perfectly retain their design.

Boil chicken, take off meat from bones, cut it into slices and season with sauce. Boil rice, add butter, cool, add chopped eggs and greens. Stew fresh boletus mushrooms in butter and season them with sauce.

Use the dough and fillings to shape a pie. For this purpose set aside ¼ of the dough for the top, roll the rest into a flat cake ¼-inch thick and put it into a greased mould or casserole allowing a piece to overlap the edges of the mould. Spread the fillings over the cake in layers as follows: rice, round slices of egg, chicken meat, mushrooms, rice again, etc., shaping the pie as a dome.

Roll the remaining dough for the top layer, make crosswise incisions on it to spread it more smoothly, and use it to cover the pie, brush it with egg and embellish with all sorts of dough flowers. Brush the surface with egg yolk again. Make a fancy-shaped opening in the centre of the dome to let out steam during baking.

Bake at 428° F. When the crust is brown, the pie is done.

Kurnik is served with a sauce. To cook it, rub butter with flour, dilute with hot broth pouring it in a steady thin stream while stirring and add cream. Heat the batter until as thick as sour cream. Take it off the heat and, stirring constantly, season with egg yolks.

Unleavened Dough

1 cup butter, ¾ cup sour cream, 1¼ cups wheat flour, a dint each of salt and sugar

Rub butter with sour cream, add salt and sugar, fill in flour and knead pliable dough.

Yeast Dough

1¼ cup butter, 2 cups milk, 1 or 2 tbsp. sugar, 1 tsp. salt, 1 egg, 30 to 50 g (1 to 1¾ oz) yeast, 6 cups wheat flour

Prepare yeast dough using the indicated ingredients, let it rise and cook pies, pasties and other baking products.

Rasstegai Pasties with Fish
(old-time recipe)

For the dough: 3 cups wheat flour, 25 g (¾ oz) fresh yeast, 2 eggs, 1/3 cup butter, 1½ cups lukewarm water, 2 tbsp. sugar, salt
For the filling: 350 to 400 g (12 to 14 oz) fillet of white fish, pike-perch or pike, 250 g (8 oz) salmon, 1 or 2 tbsp. butter, salt, ground black pepper, 1 or 2 tbsp. chopped parsley or dill
For greasing the surface: 1 or 2 eggs

Prepare yeast dough, roll it into a round strip, cut it into egg-like pieces, roll them into rounds as large as a saucer, spread the prepared fish filling on each piece and lay slices of salmon over the filling, join the opposite ends of the dough and pinch the edges leaving the centre of the pasty open. Shape the *rasstegai* into a boat, prick its surface and sides with a fork, brush with egg yolk, put on a buttered baking sheet and bake at 356° to 392° F until brown.

To prepare the fish filling, cut a fillet, sauté it in butter and season with salt, pepper and greens.

Rasstegais are *zakuska* pasties. They are served with vodka and other strong drinks, as well as with fish soup, broth or tea.

Moscow Rasstegai with Meat and Eggs
(old-time recipe)

Yeast dough: 1 kg (2 lb 3 oz)
For the filling: 800 g (1 lb 12 oz) meat, 3 tbsp. butter, 5 hard-boiled eggs, salt, ground black pepper, nutmeg
For the greasing: 2 tbsp. butter

Put the meat through a mincer or chop it by knife and sauté on a pan. Then put it through a mincer again, cool, add chopped eggs and season with salt, pepper and nutmeg. Shape dough into balls of about 150 g (5 oz), let them stay for 8 to 10 minutes and then roll into round cakes, lay the filling into the centre of each cake, build up a rim so that it overlaps the meat filling for ¾ inch, leaving the centre open. Brush up the dough rims with melted butter before and after baking. Bake at 392° F until ready.

Rasstegais are served hot with meat broth and also as a *zakuska*.

Pasties with Green Onions and Eggs

Yeast dough: 600 g (1 lb 5 oz)
For the filling: 300 g (10 oz) green onions, 3 hard-boiled eggs, 2 egg whites, 2 tbsp. melted butter, salt and
ground black pepper to taste. For the surface greasing: 2 egg yolks

Make a long roll of dough, cut it into pieces of equal size and roll them out into rounds. Put in the centre of each round the filling of minced green onions with chopped boiled eggs and one uncooked egg (for binding), and season it with salt and pepper. Pinch the edges tightly shaping the pie into a boat. Brush the surface with egg yolk and bake at 356° to 392° F.

The same method applies to pasties filled with meat, cabbage or mushrooms, but they can also be cooked by the method of deep-fat frying.

In the Russian cuisine, pasties are served in a great variety of ways: with *shchi* and *borshch*, with all kinds of soup or broth, and as a *zakuska* with vodka, kvass, tea or coffee.

Kulebyaka with Meat

Yeast dough: 700 to 800 g (1 lb 9 oz to 1 lb 12 oz)
For the filling: 1 kg (2 lb 3 oz) tender beef, 1 or 2 onions, 2 hard-boiled eggs, 2 tbsp. butter, ground black
pepper, green parsley
For the greasing: 1 or 2 egg yolks

Roll and shape the dough into an oval cake ¼-inch thick. Boil the beef, put it through a mincer, cool and add chopped eggs, slightly browned onions, salt, pepper and minced parsley. Pour melted butter and meat broth into the filling. Then pile it up on each cake, pinch the opposite edges of the dough and place on the buttered baking sheet, with its seam down, shaping it as a suckling-pig. To make the *kulebyaka* keep its shape, thicken the dough with flour on the table. To give a natural look to the pig's ears, nose and tail and to make them safely pass through a baking process, rub flour on the table into a lump of dough intended for these purposes. Attach all details made of dough to the pie by egg, and brush the surface with egg yolk – then the crust will have a good, amber-like colour. Use raisins or large peppercorns to imitate the pig's eyes. Prick the surface and sides with a fork and brush them up with the beaten yolk of egg. Bake at 410° to 426° F until ready.

The same method can be used to bake *kulebiakas* with other fillings.

FISH SOUP, SHCHI AND BORSHCH

*D*uring the reign of Ivan the Terrible, the sovereign was served, as the poet Alexei Tolstoi wrote, with three kinds of soup: white chicken soup, a black chicken variety and saffron chicken soup. A fluid part or a rich stock of poultry or fresh fish was then called *ukha*. The dish having a rhymed name, *Ukha iz petukha*, which means in fact just cock (or chicken) soup, was cooked with parsley roots, carrots and onions and was served with boneless pieces of the bird's meat. Over the time, the term *ukha* became applicable solely to a soup cooked of just caught fresh-water fish.

Royal Fish Soup

For 1 serving: 2 cups chicken broth, 50 g (1¾ oz) sturgeon, 50 g (1¾ oz) salmon, 1 onion, 1 clove garlic, salt, ground black pepper, 1 bay leaf, green dill

Drop large pieces of sturgeon and salmon into chicken broth boiled with spices and strained, bring to a boil and simmer for 15 minutes skimming off the foam. Add chopped garlic 5 minutes before ceasing to boil.

Serve sprinkled with minced greens.

Chicken Soup with Rasstegais ("Ukha iz Petukha")

It is worth trying a chicken soup with *rasstegais* or pancakes filled with chicken meat.

Boil a chicken (or better two) with 2 or 3 parsley roots, 1 carrot and 1 onion skimming off the foam. Towards the end of boiling add salt and black peppercorns. Take out the bird when done and strain the broth. Bone the meat, divide it into two parts, cut one of them into large pieces, drop into the strained broth and bring to a boil. Serve after sprinkling with minced green dill and parsley. Use the rest of the chicken meat as a filling for small *rasstegais,* pancakes or pies and serve them with the soup.

For the rasstegais: 1 kg (2 lb 3 oz) yeast dough
For the filling: 500 g (1 lb 2 oz) boneless chicken meat, 2 onions, salt, black pepper
For the greasing: 1 egg

Make a thin roll of dough, cut it into egg-sized balls and roll them out into rounds. Place in the centre of each round a filling of minced chicken meat with lightly browned onion, seasoned with salt, pepper and greens. Pinch the dough to shape it into a boat leaving the centre open. Grease with egg and bake at 356° to 392° F until golden.

Barge-Haulers' Fish Soup
(old-time recipe)

500 g (1 lb 2 oz) perches and ruffs, 200 g (7 oz) pike-perches, 4 to 5 potatoes, 2 onions, parsley sprigs, 1 tbsp. butter, ground black pepper, bay leaf

Boil broth of disembowelled perches and ruffs cleaned of gills, and strain it. Dip whole peeled potatoes and onions into the broth and continue to boil. 10 to 15 minutes before the cooking period is over, put into the fish soup pieces of pike-perch, burbot, pike or wild carp. Season the soup with salt, bay leaf, ground black pepper and boil it until ready.

Serve fish soup seasoned with butter and minced greens. The soup is good with *rasstegais* filled with fish.

Trout Soup

1 kg (2 lb 3 oz) fresh trout, 11 cups water, salt, sprigs of dill or parsley

Put into boiling salted water cleaned and disembowelled trout cut into pieces and boil, skimming off the foam, for 15 minutes. The trout soup is so savoury that it does not need any seasoning except for minced greens.

Sturgeon Soup

For 1 serving: 5 or 6 pieces of sturgeon each weighing 20 g (¾ oz), 2¼ cups fish broth, 1 onion, 1 tsp. tomato paste, 1 salted cucumber, olives, capers, black peppercorns, 1 bay leaf, slice of lemon, green dill or parsley

Shred onion, make a roux of it in butter and add tomato paste. Cut cucumbers into lozenges and sauté lightly on a pan. Scald the sturgeon, cut it into pieces and drop into a strained strong fish broth. Add the onion, cucumbers and pitted olives and boil for 10 to 15 minutes. Towards the end of boiling, dip capers, ground black pepper, bay leaf and greens.

When serving the sturgeon soup, add a slice of peeled off lemon and sprinkle with greens. Serve the soup with pies or *rasstegais*.

Cold Summer Soup

500 to 600 g (1 lb 2 oz to 1 lb 5 oz) boiled beetroot, 300 g (10 oz) fresh cucumbers, 2 or 3 hard-boiled eggs, 1 bunch each of green onions and dill, 1¼ cups sour cream, salt, sugar, lemon juice

Wash beetroot by brush, boil it unpeeled, strain and cool the broth. Shred the peeled beetroot on a coarse grater, combine with the broth, add diced cucumbers and eggs, as well as green onions and dill, season with salt, sugar and lemon juice to taste. Let the soup refrigerate for 1 hour.

Serving the cold soup, pour it into plates with sour cream, egg roundels and ice cubes.

Soup with Pickled Cucumbers and Duck Giblets

For 1 serving: duck giblets – 1 neck, 2 wings, 1 stomach, 1 heart, 1 liver; 2 potatoes, 1 salted cucumber, 1 carrot, 1 parsley root, 1 onion, vegetable oil, salt, black peppercorns, sour cream, green parsley

Use all the giblets except for the liver to boil broth. Strain the broth, drop large pieces of potatoes into it and, after bringing to a boil, add salted cucumber cut into large lozenges. Add large pieces of carrot browned lightly in butter together with onion. Then drop into the soup giblets boiled to readiness and, towards the end, add scalded and sliced liver and parsley root and bring all the ingredients to a boil. Season it to taste by salt, ground black pepper and greens and immediately remove from the heat.

Soup with giblets, a veritable delicacy, is a course for true lovers and connoisseurs of home cooking.

Potato Soup with Smelt

5 or 6 potatoes, 500 g (1 lb 2 oz) fresh smelt, 2 onions, 1 tbsp. butter, a dint of sugar, salt, black peppercorns, 1 bay leaf, green dill and parsley, sour cream

Cut potatoes into dices and drop them into boiling water. When ready, add fresh smelt. Season the soup with onions sauté until light brown with the addition of a dint of sugar, as well as salt, pepper and bay leaf.

Serve the soup with sour cream and minced greens.

A highlight of the Russian summer cuisine is *okroshka*, a cold soup based on fermented bread beverage known generally under the Russian name of kvass. In *okroshka*, kvass is combined with finely sliced meat or boiled fish, or dried, smoked or fried (boiled) game. Recipes of this soup vary depending on Russia's region: in some of them, they use salted mushrooms instead of meat or sauerkraut instead of cucumbers; sometimes fresh rice and boiled potatoes are added. Cold kvass soup is seasoned with salt, sugar, mustard and horse-radish ground with sour cream; sliced fresh cucumbers, herbs and round slices of hard-boiled eggs are also added. Let it stand in a cold place for 1 to 2 hours.

This soup is usually eaten with pies, *rasstegais* or rye bread.

Cold Kvass Soup with Fish

For 1 serving: 1¼ cups bread kvass, 50 g (1¾ oz) fish, 1 fresh cucumber, 2 tbsp. green onions, 2 tbsp. sour cream, 1 hard-boiled egg, salt, sugar, horse-radish, mustard, green dill and parsley to taste

Carve the fish into small pieces, cut cucumbers into narrow strips and chop hard-boiled eggs. Shred green onions and rub adding salt until juicy. Add into sour cream onions, mustard, salt, sugar and horse-radish, stir it up thoroughly and pour in kvass. Add to this mixture fish, eggs and finely chopped greens.

Borshch with Beans and Mushrooms

100 g (3½ oz) beans, 300 g (10 oz) beetroot, 300 g (10 oz) potatoes, 300 g (10 oz) cabbage, 50 to 60 g (1¾ to 2 oz) dried mushrooms, 1 carrot, 1 root each of parsley, celery and parsnip, 1 onion, 300 g (10 oz) fresh tomatoes or 1 to 2 tbsp. tomato paste, vegetable oil, lemon juice or table vinegar, salt and sugar to taste, 1 bunch each of dill, celery, parsley and green onions

Pour water over beans and boil them until tender and sunk to the bottom of the casserole. Add potatoes cut into bars, boil for 5 to 7 minutes, then add cabbage shredded in narrow strips. Boil mushrooms in another vessel until fully ready, strain through a colander, wash and cut like noodles, sauté in butter and add to cabbage. Strain the mushroom broth. Cut beetroot into thin slices, sprinkle with lemon juice, sauté in vegetable oil adding tomato paste and stew covered. Add the beetroot to the *borshch* and drop the other roots cut into narrow strips, without sautéing. Cut onion into half-rings, slightly sauté it and add to the *borshch*; pour in the mushroom broth. Addsalt, sugar and lemon juice to taste, at the last moment of cooking add greens and remove from the heat at once. Leave the *borshch* for 15 to 20 minutes and serve it with sour cream after sprinkling with greens.

Green Shchi or Sorrel Soup

For 1 serving: 100 g (3½ oz) leaves of sorrel, 1 fresh cucumber, green onions and dill, salt, sour cream, 1 hard-boiled egg

Green *shchi* is one of the most widespread and simple summer kinds of soup of the Russian cuisine. Mince green leaves of sorrel and drop them into boiling salted water, boil for 2 to 3 minutes, remove from the heat and cool. Pour the soup into a plate, add minced cucumber, green onions and parsley. Season with salt to taste, add sour cream and round slices of eggs.

Green *shchi* are best eaten with rye bread.

Shchi of Sauerkraut and Mushrooms

800 g (1 lb 12 oz) sauerkraut, 40 to 50 g (1½ to 1¾ oz) dried mushrooms, 2 onions, 1 root each of parsley, celery and carrot, 1 or 2 potatoes, 1 fresh tomato or 2 tbsp. tomato paste, 2 tbsp. butter, salt, sugar, green dill and parsley, sour cream

Mince sauerkraut and stew it in a covered casserole until tender adding butter, 2 or 3 tablespoons of water and a dint of sugar. Dip rinsed mushrooms into water, soak for 2 hours and boil them in the same water. Strain the mushrooms, cut as noodles, sauté in butter and add to the sauerkraut, pour in the mushroom broth. Add diced and separately boiled potatoes, shredded roots baked with tomato paste as well as slightly browned onions. Add salt and sugar, let stand for 15 to 20 minutes and serve with sour cream and minced greens.

According to age-old tradition, sour *shchi* are served with baked potato pudding with mushrooms or beef, pies, rye bread and *kalitkas* with *kasha* filling.

FISH, MEAT, GAME AND POULTRY

*R*ussian folklore is rich in vivid expressions about fish and fish courses. Its value for man's health and mood is eloquently conveyed by proverbs and sayings such as "Fish on the table means health in the home", "White fish is not large, but is good in a pie". "*Shangi* and fish soup make a conversation lively."

Fish, Monastery Style

1 kg (2 lb 3 oz) fish fillet, 500 g (1 lb 2 oz) potatoes, 300 g (10 oz) onions, 5 hard-boiled eggs, 1 cup sour cream or mayonnaise, salt, black ground pepper, green dill and parsley, flour, vegetable oil

Roll slices of fish fillet in flour mixed with salt and fry lightly on both sides in butter until brown. Sauté round slices of potatoes and onions on both sides in butter, cut hard-boiled eggs into round slices too. Place a layer of fried potatoes on a metal or silver dish, spread over it a layer of the fish cut into pieces, and arrange round slices of potatoes, onions and eggs like "scales" at the top. Add salt and pepper, pour over mayonnaise or sour cream (or sour cream with mayonnaise in equal proportions) and bake in a preheated oven until brown. The dish will be savoury and look appealing if you choose onions, potatoes and eggs similar in size.

Before serving, sprinkle the fish, monastery style, with minced greens. The fish is good with white wine.

Salmon Baked with Mushrooms

For 1 serving: 100 g (3½ oz) salmon, 1 or 2 potatoes, 40 g (1½ oz) shrimps, a handful of field mushrooms, 1 onion, 2 or 3 tbsp. mayonnaise, ground black pepper, salt, green dill and parsley, slices of lemon, olives, fresh tomatoes

Put onto the bottom of an earthenware pot potatoes cut into sections, slightly browned onions, sautéed field mushrooms and the fillet of salmon. Season it with salt and pepper, pour in mayonnaise and put shrimps above. Bake in the oven for 30 minutes.

Serve the salmon in the same pot in which it was baked, after dredging with greens, sections of fresh tomatoes, slices of lemon, and olives.

Boiled Sturgeon

For 1 serving: 150 g (5 oz) sturgeon
For the sauce: 4 tbsp. butter, 1 egg,
1 slice of lemon, salt

Cut the prepared sturgeon into portion-sized pieces (5 oz each) at an angle of 45°, boil until ready, add carrots, parsley, onions, bay leaf and salt.

Garnish with boiled potatoes, fresh cucumbers, lemon and greens. Prepare the sauce: put hard-boiled and minced eggs into melted butter, season with salt and lemon juice. Serve sturgeon with white wine.

Fried Fish

750 g (1 lb 11 oz) fish, salt, ground black pepper, flour, vegetable oil

Salt the prepared fish, pepper it, roll in flour and sauté in butter until a golden crust.

Serve with fried, boiled or mashed potatoes and salads of fresh vegetables.

47

Roasted Sturgeon

For 1 serving: 200 g (7 oz) sturgeon, 1 egg, 1 tbsp. flour, a squeeze of 1 lemon, salt, ground black pepper

Season sturgeon cut into portion-sized pieces with salt and pepper, sprinkle it with lemon juice and let it stand for 15 to 20 minutes. Then crust it in flour and roast in vegetable oil until ready. Put rounds of sautéed onions over pieces of sturgeon.

Garnish roasted sturgeon with salted cucumbers, potatoes boiled in their jackets and then peeled and fried), lemon, green lettuce and sweet red pepper.

Podvoriye Cutlets

For 2 cutlets: 150 g (5 oz) pork, 150 g (5 oz) beef, 30 g (1 oz) each of dried boletus mushrooms and field mushrooms, 1 egg, 2 onions, salt, ground black pepper, and white bread for crusting

Put the pork and beef through a mincer. Add fresh, sautéed field mushrooms and dried boletus mushrooms (previously soaked in water, cut into large lumps and sautéed after adding finely sliced onions). Then add eggs, season the minced meat with salt and pepper, mix thoroughly and shape into round cutlets. Crust in diced white bread, sauté on both sides and bake until ready in the oven.

Garnish with green pies, fried potatoes, sweet pepper, fresh cucumbers and olives. Decorate with sautéed field mushrooms, a tomato shaped as a flower and sprigs of curly parsley.

Serve the Podvoriye Cutlets with red wine or Russian vodka.

Sausages, Podvoriye Restaurant Style

For 1 serving: 500 g (1 lb 2 oz) pork, 20 g (¾ oz) smoked lard, salt, black peppercorns, clove garlic

The Podvoriye Sausages are cooked according to the long-established technology. Divide pork into two parts, put one of them through a mincer, and chop the other with a knife. Also chop lard, mix it with the pork, add minced garlic, ground black pepper and salt, combine all the ingredients adding 2 or 3 tablespoons water to make the mixture juicy, and if the pork is lean, it is desirable to add 15 to 20 g (½ to ¾ oz) lard (per serving), in addition to the smoked one. Mix the ingredients and fill the prepared intestines with the minced meat, turn each sausage in a ring, tie its ends with a thread and fry on both sides until brown, pouring it with pork drippings or with dry wine.

Garnish the hot pork sausage with potatoes cooked in their jackets and then peeled and fried, stewed cabbage with salted mushrooms, salad of green vegetables and olives.

Beef Stroganoff

Beef Stroganoff, a meat dish in sour cream and tomato sauce, has entered cookbooks in many countries thanks to Baron and Count Alexander G. Stroganoff, a prominent representative of the Stroganoff family.

For 1 serving: 150 g (5 oz) beef, 1 small onion, 1/3 cup sauce

Pound a lump of fillet beef with mallet until thin and cut it into strips 2 to 2½-inch long and ½-inch thick. Then cut them crosswise into bits ¼ to ½ inch, add salt and pepper and sauté, stirring occasionally. Add minced onions and continue to sauté until ready. Prepare a sauce of sour cream and tomatoes, make a roux of 2 tablespoons of flour in 3 tablespoons of tomato paste and continue to fry, then pour in 1 cup of sour cream, season with salt, black ground pepper, add a chopped clove of garlic, minced parsley and dill sprigs, stir and bring to a boil.

Serve the dish hot with fried or boiled potatoes cut into slices and sautéed, green peas, fresh cucumbers and tomatoes.

Home-Made Cutlets

300 g (10 oz) beef, 200 g (7 oz) pork, 2 onions, 2 lumps of white bread, salt, black ground pepper, 2 tbsp. frying fat

Put beef, pork, onions and white bread soaked in milk or water and wrought out through a mincer; add salt and pepper, stir up, shape into cutlets and fry until brown.

Serve with fresh tomatoes, cucumbers, pickled plums, green lettuce, parsley and dill.

Hunter's Cutlets of Elk's Meat

For 1 serving (2 cutlets): 260 g (9 oz) elk's meat, 1 tbsp. butter, salt, black peppercorns, bay leaf, vinegar

Put in advance a lump of elk's meat into hot boiled water, add vinegar, bay leaf, black peppercorns and pickle and let it stand for 4 to 8 hours. Then put the meat through a mincer, add to the minced meat butter or lard, season it with salt and pepper, stirring well and shaping into round cutlets.

Bake cutlets in a hot pan until a golden crust, then bringing the dish to complete readiness in the oven.

Serve the Hunter's Cutlets with a mixed garnish: lettuce, fresh cucumbers and tomatoes, salted white mushrooms, salad of finely chopped strips of cabbage, pies, olives and green parsley.

Russian Roast

300 g (10 oz) beef, 3 to 4 potatoes, 2 tbsp. butter, 1 carrot, 1 root each of parsley and celery, 1 onion, 2 cloves garlic, 1 to 2 tbsp. sour cream, salt, 1 bay leaf, black peppercorns, green parsley or dill

Sauté the beef cut into pieces in butter until light brown. Cut potatoes into dices, onions into rings and roots in narrow strips and fry them separately. Put the beef, potatoes, onions and roots into a pot and season with salt, pepper, bay leaf, add a little broth and stew in the oven for 30 minutes covered. Some 10 minutes before the end of cooking add sour cream to the roast. Sprinkle the ready roast with minced garlic, cover and take the cover off at once. Serve after sprinkling the dish with greens.

Mutton Cutlets

For 1 serving (2 cutlets): 100 g (3½ oz) mutton, 1 egg, 1 onion, 1 clove garlic, lemon juice

Put mutton through a mincer, add salt, lemon juice, an egg and carefully stir up the minced meat. Shape into oval cutlets and bake in the oven for no more than 20 minutes. It is important not to overcook them there, since otherwise they will be too dry.

Served with a salad of sauerkraut, sliced salted cucumbers and olives.

Shashlyk

1 kg (2 lb 3 oz) lean pork, 6 or 7 onions, salt, black ground paper, lemon juice

   Cut pork into pieces each weighing about 15 to 20 g (½ to ¾ oz), sprinkle them with lemon juice, salt and pepper and put into an enamel vessel (better in an earthenware pot), scatter onion rings, mix up, put a load over the mixture and refrigerate for 6 to 8 hours. Thread pieces of pork on to metal spits alternating with rings of onions, and roast on an electric grill, in a gas or electric oven, but the best result is achieved on coals. Mind that the coals should have already been burnt.
   Serve *shashlyks* with fresh vegetables and abundant greens (dill, parsley, basil, cress and coriander).

Stuffed Partridge

For 1 serving: 1 partridge, half an apple, 2 to 3 tbsp. red whortleberry, salt and pepper

Rub the prepared bird with salt and pepper, fill with the diced apple mixed with the red whortleberry. Rub the partridge with softened butter and tie the legs with a cord. Roast in the oven until brown.

Garnish with canned fruit, soaked red whortleberry, paradise apples, fresh vegetables, olives, herbs and lettuce.

Serve with red wine.

Rabbit Roast in Red Wine

For 1 serving: 2 legs of rabbit, 75 g (2 ½ oz) potatoes, 1 onion, 15 g (½ oz) dried boletus mushrooms or 30 g (1 oz) field mushrooms, 1 cup red wine, salt, 1 tsp. tomato paste, green dill and parsley

Put the potatoes cut in large pieces into a pot or other ceramic vessel. Cut the legs of rabbit, fry in butter until half-ready and add to the potatoes. Sauté onions and mushrooms, add to the potatoes and rabbit and pour with a red wine. Season the roast with the sautéed tomato paste and salt and stew until ready.

The rabbit roast is good with soaked red whortleberry and greens.

Elk's Meat Roast

Pickle elk's meat in hot water, after adding vinegar, bay leaf and black peppercorns, for 4 to 8 hours. Cut the meat into portions (4 pieces per portion of 150 g [5 oz]) and smoke in a home smoking-shed. Add water and braise the slightly smoked meat for an hour. Cut carrots into small pieces and sauté them together with rings of onions, add tomato paste and continue to fry. Put potatoes cut into large pieces and stew together with carrots and onions. Add the vegetables to the elk meat and roast until ready. Serve the roast seasoned with salt and spices in earthenware vessels.

Flavoury Fillet

For 1 serving: 200 g (7 oz) loin of pork, ¼ cup red grape wine

Pound the pork along the tissues and pierce a little with a small mallet, sprinkle with lemon juice, add salt, pepper, sauté in a very hot pan on both sides until a golden crust, together with large rings of onions. Then reduce heat and pour in red wine so that the pork has soaked and become flavoury.

Garnish the fillet with fresh cucumbers and tomatoes, soaked red whortleberry and sauerkraut salad.

Duck with Sauerkraut

For 2 servings: duck weighing 1 kg (2 lb 3 oz), 500 g (1 lb 2 oz) stewed sauerkraut, 1 onion, vegetable oil, 2 tbsp. sour cream, a handful of prunes, black pepper, salt, sugar, bay leaf

Cut the bird lengthwise into two parts, pound it with a mallet, add salt and pepper and sauté in the oven until golden, then add 2 to 3 tablespoons of water and simmer covered for 25 to 30 minutes.

Stew sauerkraut with 1 cup of broth or water adding sautéed onions, continue to simmer covered. 5 to 7 minutes before the sauerkraut is ready, add prunes, sour cream, salt, pepper and bay leaf.

Serve the duck with sauerkraut, boiled potatoes, baked apples with soaked red whortleberry, fresh cucumbers, lettuce, red sweet pepper and slices of lemon.

CEREALS, PASTA POACHES AND OMELETTES

*F*or centuries cereals or *kashas* were a common staple of the Russian people. Meanwhile cereals are not only a variety of nourishing courses, but a ritual dish as well. Several peoples in this country used to cook a cereal known as "granny's *kasha*" to mark the birth of a baby. The bridegroom and the bride were supposed to cook a cereal as part of their wedding ceremony, hence the popular saying: "You won't cook a cereal with him (or with her)," meaning that he or she is not good as a partner. A special cereal (*kutya*) was cooked for a funeral repast. It could not be otherwise with the people whose diet has long been based on bread and grain as is reflected in popular Russian sayings and proverbs: "Buckwheat *kasha* is our mother, and brown bread is our dear father", "*Borshch* is but a widower without buckwheat *kasha*, and *kasha* is a widow without *borshch*."

After *shchi* and *kasha*, pasta poaches (*pelmeni*) are perhaps the most popular course of the Russian cuisine, and it is definitely a staple with the inhabitants of the Urals and Siberia.

Pearl Barley Kasha with Cracklings

Man's thankful attitude to his daily bread is expressed in beautiful and tender names given to dishes. Take, for example, a pearl barley *kasha*. It is not a mere chance that the world "pearl" is present in its name. The dish bearing such a poetic name came to us from the distant past.

To boil pearl barley *kasha*, you need: 1 cup pearl barley, 2 cups water, salt and butter. Sort out and clean pearl barley, wash it changing water seven times, put into a clay pot and let it soak overnight. In the morning, salt it, stir and bring to a boil, add 1 or 2 tablespoons of butter and cook for 15 to 20 minutes covered over a low heat or in the oven. The *kasha* of pearl barley soaked in advance takes less time to cook and has an appearance of true pearls – each grain separate from another.

The traditional Russian stove was the heart of the Russian peasant home. It would, metaphorically speaking, like mother, cook food, warm and wash you, would put you to bed and cure from fever.

Millet Kasha

2 cups millet, 2 cups water, 2 cups milk, salt, sugar, butter

Sort out millet and wash it changing water seven times. When water after washing is transparent and the millet is absolutely clean, pour over hot water and evaporate it quickly, season with salt and a dash of sugar. Pour over hot milk, stir and place the pot into the oven. When *kasha* is well stewed and has a golden crust, it can be served to the table with butter and milk.

Potato Kasha with Cracklings

1 kg (2 lb 3 oz) crumbly potatoes, 1 egg, 100 to 150 g (3½ to 5 oz) lard, 2 onions, salt

Pour hot water over peeled potatoes, add salt and boil until ready. Drain off water and crush the potatoes thoroughly adding egg. Sauté diced lard at a moderate heat until golden cracklings begin to form. Separate the cracklings and use the melted lard to sauté onions cut into rings. Combine them with the potatoes, stir and place the mixture on a serving dish. Scatter the glowing cracklings and onion rings on the top. Serve the *kasha* hot as an independent course with salted cucumbers, soaked apples, and red whortleberries, sauerkraut and salad of fresh vegetables.

Buckwheat Kasha

1 cup buckwheat groats, 2 cups water, salt

Sort out buckwheat groats, remove flour dust, slightly dry on a pan stirring frequently and drop the groats into a pot, add salt, pour in water, cover and boil in the oven until ready. *Kasha* should be crispy and have a red-brownish tinge. It is best eaten with milk, oil and seasoned with fried onions.

Another method of cooking the *kasha* is as follows: wash the groats changing water seven times, pour in cold water and bring to a boil. Drain off the liquid and pour boiling water over the groats again, add salt and, if desired, a dint of sugar. Cover the pot and bring the *kasha* to complete readiness in the oven. This *kasha* has a tender taste, light colour and subtle fragrance. It is served with honey, milk or butter.

Baked Cottage Cheese Pudding

1 cup cottage cheese, 1 egg, 1 tsp. sugar, a dint each of salt and soda, 1 tbsp. semolina, 1 tbsp. candied orange peel or a handful of raisins, 1 tbsp. butter, 1 tbsp. bread crumbs

Rub cottage cheese with salt, sugar and egg, add semolina and soda, stir until well blended and spread as an even coat in a buttered mould or pan sprinkled with bread crumbs. Bake in a 356° to 392° F oven until brown. Serve the fritter with sour cream, honey, jam, cranberry or currants ground with sugar, for tea and coffee.

Omelette Baked in the Oven

3 eggs, 4 or 5 tbsp. milk, a dint of salt, 1 tbsp. butter, 1 tsp. grated cheese, green dill

Shake eggs with salt until frothy and pour over milk without ceasing to shake. Pour the mixture into a preheated pan with melted butter and sprinkle with cheese. Bake omelette in the oven for 20 minutes, which is somewhat longer than frying it on the stove, but a fried version cannot rival it in airiness and soft taste. Serve the omelette when the crust begins to brown, after sprinkling it with minced dill.

Cottage Cheese Fritters

1 cup cottage cheese, 1 egg, 1 tbsp. sugar, a dint each of salt and soda, 2 tbsp. wheat flour, 2 tbsp. butter for frying

Rub cottage cheese with salt, sugar and egg until well blended, add flour with soda, knead the cottage cheese batter, roll it into a round strip, cut into pieces and give them an oval or round shape, sauté in butter on both sides until brown. Serve the fritters hot with sour cream and jam for tea, coffee or milk.

Pelmeni (Pasta Poaches) with Meat Filling

For the dough: 6 cups wheat flour, 2 cups water, salt
For the minced meat: 300 g (10 oz) each of beef, pork fat, mutton and white meat of chicken or turkey-hen, 2 onions, 2 cloves garlic, ground black pepper, bay leaf, nutmeg, salt, cream or milk

To prepare dough, sift flour shaping a mound, make a depression in it, pour in water, salt and carefully mix up water with flour. Better rotate the dough in the same direction to make it resilient and pliable. Roll the dough into a tight ball and let it rest for 20 minutes covered by a wet napkin, to evade drying. Prepare minced meat putting it through a mincer twice. Add minced onions, ground black pepper, bay leaf, nutmeg, salt and enough fresh cream, milk or water to make the filling succulent. Form meat balls. Shape the dough as a roll, cut it into pieces equal to the meat balls, roll them out into thin rounds, place pieces of meat in the centre of each round of dough and securely seal them by pinching. Drop the pinched poaches into a boiling meat stock or into water adding 1 or 2 meat or mushroom bouillon cubes or just into salted water. To improve the flavour and taste of *pelmeni*, add to the stock black peppercorns, bay leaf or an onion. When the pasta poaches emerge from the liquid, they are done.

Pasta poaches may have different fillings: potatoes, green onions, radish, fresh cabbage, sauerkraut, mushrooms, fish or omelette.

Pelmeni can also be cooked over a steam, fried in oil or stewed with sour cream in a ceramic pot sealed with a puff paste and placed into the oven. (In the popular cuisine, *pelmeni* are served in their own stock.) Serve *pelmeni* hot with butter, sour cream, vinegar and lemon juice, sprinkled with grated cheese or finely chopped greens.

Pelmeni with Fish Filling

For the dough: 6 cups wheat flour
For the minced fish: 1 kg (2 lb 3 oz) fillet of Siberian, hunchback or other kind of salmon, 1 onion, 100 g (3½ oz) lard or pork fat, 1 egg, a dint of sugar, salt, ground black pepper

Cut the fillet of fish and put through a mincer twice together with onions and lard. Add an egg, cream or milk, sugar, salt and pepper and stir well to make the filling uniform, succulent and binding. Spread pieces of the fish filling on rolled out rounds of dough, shape pasta poaches and boil for no less than 15 minutes.

Serve with butter and sour cream and sprinkled with finely minced green parsley or grated strong cheese.

POTATOES, VEGETABLES AND MUSHROOMS

*P*otatoes are a staple food in the Russian cuisine. Boiled, fried or mashed potatoes, potatoes cooked in their jackets and then peeled and fried, potatoes served with herring, salted or pickled mushrooms, sauerkraut, with crispy cracklings or soaked red whortleberry (Novgorod style), with lard and a juicy bulb of onion or, better, a clove of garlic, potatoes steamed with chanterelles and dill, potato fritters with mushrooms or meat, dumplings— you cannot even enumerate all dishes based on potatoes. This simple and exquisite traditional fare is always desirable at our tables both on festive occasions and in everyday life.

Potatoes Stewed with Cream

1 to 1.5 kg (2 lb 3 to 3 lb 5 oz) potatoes, 1 cup cream, 2 umbels of young dill, salt

Drop thinly sliced potatoes into an earthenware or cast-iron pot, season with salt and minced dill and pour over cream. Cover the pot and toss it to blend the cream well with the potatoes; place in the oven and stew until ready. Best served with a salad of fresh cucumbers and tomatoes.

This dish is extremely tasty and worthy to be enjoyed by real gourmets.

Milk Saffron Caps Fried in Butter

Slice milk saffron caps sauté in butter, roll them in flour mixed with salt and fry on both sides in butter. This Russian delicacy has no rivals as regards its taste and flavour.

Draniki *(Potato Pancakes)*

12 medium-sized potatoes, 1 tbsp. sour cream or milk, 2 tbsp. wheat flour, salt, vegetable oil

Peel potatoes, grate them, add sour cream, flour and salt and mix all the ingredients. Place the potato mixture in a strongly preheated pan with vegetable oil and sauté the pancakes on both sides until a brown crust appears.

Draniki are best eaten hot with cracklings, sour cream, soaked red whortleberry, sprinkled with garlic and green onions and accompanied by beer.

Honey Agarics Fried in Sour Cream

2 cups fresh honey agarics, 2 tbsp. butter, ¾ cup sour cream, 2 onions, salt, green dill and parsley

Place cleaned and washed honey agarics in boiling salted water and cook for 3 to 4 minutes, strain through a colander, cut into narrow strips, fry in butter, add sautéed onions and salt, pour over sour cream and bring to readiness.

Serve as a hot *zakuska* sprinkled with greens. This method of cooking applies to any other kind of mushrooms.

Potatoes Stewed with Chanterelles

For 1 serving: 500 g (1 lb 2 oz) potatoes, 300 g (10 oz) mushrooms (chanterelles), 2 onions, 3 tbsp. butter, green onions and dill

Boil potatoes cut into large pieces in a pot until ready, drain off the liquid leaving a little at the bottom. Combine the potatoes with chanterelles sautéed in butter together with onions. Add salt and minced dill and stew in the oven until ready.

Best eaten with dill, green onions and kvass. If desired, it may be accompanied by soaked red whortleberry.

As a Russian saying goes, "One who has never picked up mushrooms hasn't seen the world." And the Russian festive table is unthinkable without mushrooms – these dishes include wedding kurniks with boletus mushrooms (these favourites are known as "white" mushrooms in Russia) and stewed potatoes with chanterelles, not to mention the king of zakuskas, salted saffron milk-caps in sour cream!

Potato Pie with Meat Filling

For the mashed potatoes: 10 to 12 large potatoes, 2 eggs, 2 or 3 tbsp. butter, 4 tbsp. thick sour cream, salt
For the filling: 400 to 500 g (14 oz to 1 lb 2 oz) boiled meat, 1 or 2 onions, 2 tbsp. butter, ground black pepper, nutmeg, salt

Boil peeled potatoes and mash them. Add eggs and mix with the mashed potatoes until fluffy and creamy. Add butter, sour cream and salt. Place the mashed potatoes on a buttered pan in an even layer and lay meat filling made of ground boiled meat mixed with sauté onions and seasoned with salt, pepper and nutmeg. Over it, along the edge of the pie, make a border pattern in mashed potatoes with the help of a bag, leaving the centre open. Bake the pie.

Serve as an independent course with soaked paradise apples, red whortleberry and home-made salted dainties.

Carrots in Milk Sauce

500 g (1 lb 2 oz) carrots, 1 tsp. sugar, a dint of salt, a walnut-sized lump of butter
For the milk sauce: 2 cups milk, 1 tbsp. wheat flour, 2 tbsp. butter, salt

Cut prepared carrots into dices or rounds, pour over water or bouillon, season with salt and sugar and blanch until ready, when nearly all the liquid evaporates. Pour milk sauce over the carrots, bring to a boil and cook for 5 to 7 minutes.

For the sauce, make a roux of flour in butter until light yellow, pour hot milk in a steady thin stream stirring constantly, add sugar and salt to taste and bring to a boil.

Carrots Stewed with Mutton

1 kg (2 lb 3 oz) carrots, 500 g (1 lb 2 oz) young mutton, 2 tbsp. butter, 2 onion, sugar to taste, 7 to 10 ground black peppercorns, 2 or 3 bay leaves

Cut mutton into small pieces and sauté in a buttered deep vessel. When the mutton browns, add minced onions, a dint of sugar and continue to sauté until the onion becomes golden-coloured. Then add carrots cut into round slices, pour over hot water or bouillon, and bring to a boil. Reduce heat and stew covered until ready. 5 to 7 minutes before the end of stewing, season with salt, sugar, pepper and bay leaf to taste.

Fried Pumpkin

200 g (7 oz) pumpkin, vegetable oil, green parsley

After peeling and removing seeds cut pumpkin into slices, add salt and fry in oil.

Serve lavishly sprinkled with minced parsley.

Beetroot with Sour Cream

150 g (5 oz) beetroot, 3 tbsp. sour cream, salt, green dill, parsley and onions

Young beetroot has a bright colour and tender taste and is especially savoury with sour cream. Peel boiled beetroot, slice it and serve with sour cream and herbs or green onions.

TEA-DRINKING, RUSSIAN STYLE

*T*ea-drinking with honey cakes, gingerbread, pies, cookies and *blinis* is a national custom popular in every Russian household. The growth of land-ploughing and bee-keeping promoted the development of a honey cake cooking craft. Honey cakes were a popular pastry with all layers of society, as well as a token of benevolence and hospitality and a desirable gift. Therefore the honey cake as a form of folk handicraft, and just as a savoury culinary product, despite of its short "life", has certainly assimilated all styles and fashions. Nowadays, many families have still preserved a fine tradition to make honey cakes given as presents for Christmas and Easter and family holidays. The best-loved version is a heart-shaped honey cake symbolizing a sincere affection. Sometimes honey cakes bear dedicatory inscriptions such as "To our dear Masha" or "To our dear Ivan". Boys are usually presented with a cake in the shape of a cockerel, horse or deer, while girls' usual gifts are items shaped as a doll, a Russian *matrioshka* or a toy bird. A young couple used to receive a honey cake shaped as a cradle. Honey cakes have still remained traditional presents symbolizing happy and rich life.

Vatrushkas
(Open Cottage Cheese or Jam Cakes)

Yeast dough: 600 to 700 g (1 lb 5 oz to 1 lb 9 oz)
For the filling: 2 or 3 tbsp. dense apple, plum or apricot jam, dry apricots, cottage cheese
For the greasing: 1 egg

Shape dough into a roll, cut it into pieces about 50 g (1¾ oz) each, shape them into flat round cakes and put on the buttered baking sheet. Let the dough rise for 15 to 20 minutes, then make a depression in the centre of each cake and fill it with cottage cheese, dried apricots, jam or berries. Bake at 356° to 392° F.

Serve with tea or coffee.

Shangi
(Vatrushkas with Mashed Potatoes)

Yeast dough: 600 to 700 g (1 lb 5 oz to 1 lb 9 oz)
For the filling: 7 or 8 potatoes, 1 egg, 1 egg white, 2 tbsp. each of sour cream and vegetable oil, salt to taste
For the greasing: 1 egg yolk

Roll dough into a rope and slice it into pieces of about 50 g (1¾ oz) each. Roll the pieces into balls, place on a greased baking sheet and let them stand for 15 to 20 minutes. Make a depression in the centre of each piece, fill it with beaten up mashed potatoes and egg using a bag. Bake at 392° F until brown. Serve with various soups, kvass or tea.

There is a mysterious attraction in a tea-drinking party when people gather around a traditional Russian tea urn called samovar. Each true samovar heated by burning coals seems to have its own voice. It is probably the samovar's pleasant and appeasing melody that builds up primarily a very special friendly atmosphere inviting for tea-drinking.

Kalitkas *(Rye Vatrushkas)*

Kalitkas are small open rye pies with fillings of cereals, flour, mashed potatoes or vegetables.

A dough for *kalitkas* is made of rye flour or a mixture of rye and wheat flours in equal proportions, according to the following recipe: 2 cups flour, 1 cup liquid (water, milk, sour milk or sour cream in any proportions), a dint of salt.

Let the dough rest for 20 to 30 minutes covered by a napkin. Roll the dough into a round strip, cut it into equal pieces, shape into balls, roll them into thin rounds. Spread on them all kinds of fillings and pinch or fold up the edges. Bake at 356° to 392° F. Serve with *shchi*, tea, coffee or milk.

Lemon Pie

Yeast dough: 700 to 800 g (1 lb 9 oz to 1 lb 12 oz)
For the filling: 2 large thick-skinned lemons, 4 or 5 tbsp. sugar, 1 tbsp. starch, 2 tbsp. bread crumbs

Roll dough into a round no less than ½-inch thick, place it in a mould greased with vegetable oil and prick the bottom with a fork. Sprinkle bread crumbs in an even layer over the dough surface and top it with lemon filling. Build up a rim about ¾ inch above the level of the dough. Embellish the border of the pie with leaves and flowers made of dough, if desired. Grease the surface with egg or tea. Bake at 356° to 392° F.

To prepare the filling, wash and dry lemons, shred them on a fine grater together with peels but removing seeds for otherwise the filling will be bitter. Add sugar and starch and mix it.

Serve with tea or coffee.

Roses

Yeast dough: 1 kg (2 lb 3 oz)
For the greasing: ¾ cup butter
For sprinkling the cakes:
for the cheese "roses" – 1½ cups grated cheese;
for cinnamon "roses" – 1 tbsp. cinnamon, 2 tbsp. sugar, a handful each of raisins and nuts;
for the poppy-seed "roses" – 2 tbsp. poppy-seed, 2 tbsp. sugar, a handful each of raisins and walnuts

Roll dough into an oblong ¼ to ½-inch thick, grease with butter, sprinkle with cheese shredded on a medium grater, form into a roll, pinch the seam along the roll and slice it into pieces 1 to 1¼-inch wide. Then, pinching each piece on one side to make its bottom, unfold dough "petals" shaping them like a rose flower. Place the "roses", with their bottoms down, on a baking sheet greased with oil and bake at 356° to 392° F until brown. After removing, sprinkle them with melted butter and serve at the table.

The same method can be used to produce "roses" with poppy-seed, raisins or walnuts, as well as with cinnamon, sugar, raisins or nuts.

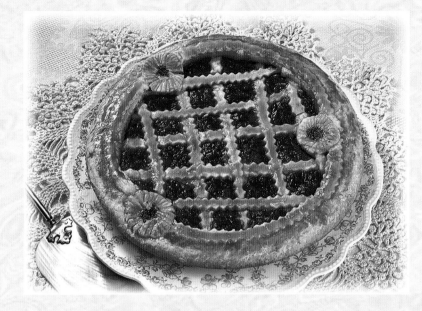

Pie with Red Whortleberry Jam

Unleavened dough: 800 g (1 lb 12 oz)
For the filling: 400 g (14 oz) thick red whortleberry jam
For the greasing: 1 egg

Roll out the dough into a flat round and place it on a pie pan or in a round mould setting aside about 1/5 of the dough for a decorative lattice and flowers. Place an even layer of jam over the dough and build up the rim of the pie. Roll out the remaining dough into a very thin cake and cut it into zigzag-shaped strips with a corrugated knife. Place them crisscross over jam concealing their edges and the rim of the pie by a similar zigzag-shaped strip of dough. Adorn the pie with flowers and grease with egg. Bake pie at 356° to 410° F until brown.

Rolled Cake with Cinnamon and Raisins

Yeast dough: 1 kg (2 lb 3 oz)
For the filling: 1 tbsp. ground cinnamon, 2 tbsp. sugar, a handful each of chopped walnuts and raisins
For the dressing: 1 tsp. confectioners' sugar

Roll out dough into an oblong and sprinkle it evenly with a blend of cinnamon, sugar, walnut meat and raisins. Roll the dough up, firmly pinch the seam along the roll and place in a buttered cake mould with corrugated edges and a pipe in the middle. Bring together the edges of the roll, pinch the seam, prick the surface with a fork, let the dough stand for some time to rise almost level with the edges of the mould and bake it at 356° to 392° F until brown. Let the rolled cake completely chill and take it out of the mould and sprinkle it with confectioners' sugar.

Name-Day Cake

For the dough: 2½ cups wheat flour, 2¼ cups butter, 2 cups sugar, 8 egg yolks, a handful each of raisins and chopped walnuts, 1 tbsp. candied orange peel, a dint of soda and salt, lemon juice
For the custard: 2 egg yolks, ½ cup confectioners' sugar

Rub butter with a half of sugar until crystals completely disappear. Rub egg yolks separately with the remaining sugar and combine both mixtures. Add raisins, nuts, candied orange peel, soda, several drops of lemon juice and salt. Blend all the ingredients, add flour and quickly knead light and fluffy dough of consistently uniform quality. Place the dough in a buttered tin filling it to ¾ volume and put in a 356° F oven gently. Bake until ready for about 50 minutes. Chill the baked cake and take it out of the mould.

Whip a custard of egg whites and sugar and decorate the cake with small flowers using a bag. If desired, the cake can be put into the warm oven for several minutes to lend the custard a colour of tea-rose. Adorn the cake with burning candles.

Cake: Rosen (Rosettes)

Yeast dough: 600 g (1 lb 5 oz)
For the filling: 2 or 3 tbsp. poppy-seed, 1 or 2 tbsp. sugar, 2 tbsp. melted butter

Roll the dough into an oblong ¼ to ½-inch thick, butter it, sprinkle with poppy-seed and sugar, roll the cake and firmly pinch the seam. Cut the cake crosswise into pieces ¾-inch wide, pinch on the one side and shape all the pieces like roses. Place the roses into a round mould combining them to form a "bouquet". Bake the pie at 356° F.

Serve the cake for coffee and tea.

Cookies: The Forest Tale

For the dough: 2 cups wheat flour, 1¼ cups butter, ½ cup sugar, 4 eggs, 0.5 tsp. soda, 1 tsp. lemon juice, a dint of salt and vanilla
For the trimming: jam of wild berries

Rub butter with a half of sugar adding egg yolks, one at a time, and then salt, soda, lemon juice and vanilla. Mix all the ingredients, top the prepared mixture with sifted flour and add egg whites beaten up with the remaining sugar until frothy. Knead smooth light dough stirring it from top to bottom. Syringe the dough shaped into flowers onto buttered metal sheets. Make small depressions in the middle of each flower and fill it with a jam of forest berries – red whortleberry, bilberry, cranberry, cloudberry, raspberry or blackberry. Bake at 392° F until light brown.

The Forest Tale is fascinating for its bright play of colours and the charming gamut of flavours. Serve the cookies for tea or coffee.

Boris Kustodiev. Merchant's Wife. 1912. The Russian Museum, St Petersburg

How can tea-drinking do without jam? Tea with jam, *blinis* with jam and *vatrushkas* with jam are invariable attributes of the Russian tea table.

Blackberry Jam

1 kg (2 lb 3 oz) blackberry, 6 cups sugar

Sort out ripe solid blackberries picked up on a dry day. Before boiling, fill the berries with a half of the sugar and leave in a cool place until juicy. Then mix the juice with the remaining sugar, bring to a boil, add the berries and boil until ready shaking the basin occasionally by rotating movements and skimming off the foam. Chill the ready jam quickly by dipping the basin into cold water and put the jam into glass jars.

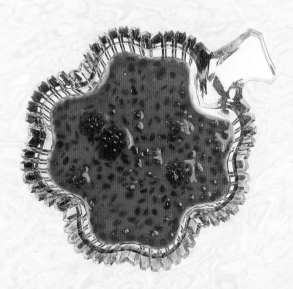

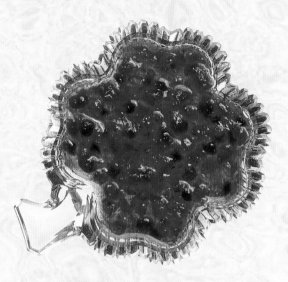

and boil skimming off the foam. 10 minutes before finishing to boil, add the apricot kernels.

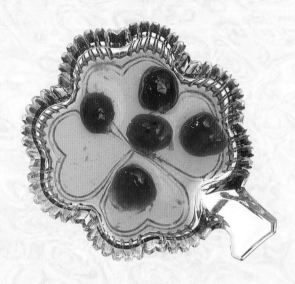

Red Whortleberry Jam

1 kg (2 lb 3 oz) red whortleberry, 5 cups sugar, 1½ cups water

Boil sugar syrup, add washed and dried berries and cook, skimming off the foam, until ready. Put into jars and leave until completely chilled. Then close with covers or parchment paper.

Cherry Jam

1 kg (2 lb 3 oz) cherries, 5 cups sugar, 2 cups water

Wash sorted out and cleaned berries in cold water, remove pits, put into a vessel in layers sprinkling each layer with sugar and keep for several hours until juicy. Shift the berries into a basin and pour in the rest of the sugar washed off by water. Put the basin with berries over a heat and bring it to a boil stirring constantly. Simmer until ready without an interval, skimming off the foam regularly.

Apricot Jam

1 kg (2 lb 3 oz) apricots, 7 cups sugar, 2 cups water, a handful of apricot kernels

Cut washed apricots lengthwise, remove pits and take out their kernels. Blanch the apricots in boiling water for 1 minute, quickly chill, fill with sugar syrup

Pie with Dried Apricots

Yeast dough: 1 kg (2 lb 3 oz)
For the filling: 1 kg (2 lb 3 oz) choicest dried apricots, ¾ cup sugar

Roll dough into an oval and prick its surface with a fork. Place pieces of dried apricots in an even layer, bend the wedge of the dough, grease it with the syrup in which the apricots were boiled, decorate it with dough flowers also greased with the syrup, and drop poppy-seed into the centre of each flower. To prepare the dried apricots intended for the filling, put them into water so that it just covers the berries, fill in sugar and blanch slightly until half-tender. Put the apricots on the sieve allowing the syrup to drain and cooling the apricots.

Bake the pie at 356° to 392° F until ready. Brush the rim of the cooked pie and pieces of dried apricots with syrup again. The pie has a pleasant sour-sweet taste and magnificent flavour. Serve for tea or coffee.

Cookies: Festive Present

For the dough: 2 cups flour, 1¼ cups butter, ¾ cup sugar, 2 eggs, 0.5 tsp. soda, a half of grated lemon with peel, a dint of salt
For the greasing: 2 egg yolks
For the filling: 1 tbsp. jam each of apricot, apple, plum, cherry, peach and cranberry varieties, cottage cheese
For the icing: white and chocolate glaze

Prepare dough, roll it and cut out flat cakes using a round tin with a corrugated edge. Make a depression in each of the cakes and fill them with various thick jams. Brush the surface around jam with egg yolks. Bake the cookies at 392° F until golden-brown, chill and paint with white and chocolate glazes.

Cake: Swallow's Nest

For the base of the cake: 8 egg yolks, 2 cups sugar
For the custard: 2¾ cups butter, 1 cup confectioners' sugar, 5 egg yolks, 2 tbsp. black Riga balsam
For the trimming: mocha chocolate coffee bean and chocolate streusel

Beat off chilled egg whites until frothy and pour in sugar by a steady thin stream without ceasing to beat off. Divide the egg whites into two parts and use the first one to bake three pie shells. Syringe the remaining part shaped into small flowers onto a baking sheet covered with a paper. Bake them at more than 212° F until the colour of tea-rose.

Whip a custard of fresh butter with gradual addition of confectioners' sugar and egg yolks. Flavour the custard with Riga balsam.

Grease the chilled pie shells with the custard, place them one over another and grease the upper and lateral sides of the cake. Adorn the side surface with small dough flowers and the top with chocolate coffee beans and chocolate streusel.

Honey Cakes:
The Humpbacked Horse

For the dough: 3 cups rye flour, 2 tbsp. butter, 500 g (1 lb 2 oz) honey, 1 egg, 1 tsp. ground spices (cinnamon, cloves, cardamom, anise and ginger), 1 tsp. each soda and lemon juice, a dint of salt
For the chocolate glazing: ¾ cup confectioners' sugar, 2 tbsp. powdered cacao, 3 tbsp. hot water, 2 tbsp. melted butter
For the white glazing: 1 egg white, ¾ cup confectioners' sugar

Melt butter, mix it with honey and egg, add minced spices, soda, lemon juice and flour, knead dough and let it rest. Then roll the dough, cut out the figurines of horses by a special cutter, bake them, glaze and decorate with painted patterns.

According to the long-established tradition, the honey cakes *Horse, Deer* and *The Red-Combed Cockerel* were given as presents to boys and youths as symbols of manhood.

94

From time immemorial the artists of Palekh painted icons. This well-known school of lofty and exquisite art can be sensed in all subjects of decorative articles produced in this centre.

LENTEN FARE

*T*emperance in food has always been characteristic of all the strata of Russian society. The Russian Orthodox people who strictly observed fasts had an excellent health, both physically and morally. The alternation of numerous fasts and festivals shaped the Russian mode of life.

E. A. Avdeyeva wrote in her *Handbook of the Russian Experienced Housewife*, published in 1845: "Not denying either the German or French cuisine, I believe that for us, the Russians, our native cookery is more healthy and useful in all aspects. We are accustomed to it, it relies on the century-old traditions and has been handed down from fathers to children; it can be accounted for by our environment, climate and mode of life. It is good to borrow positive things from abroad, but we should not neglect our own experience and it must always serve as a basis for us."

Cabbage Salad with Cranberry

300 g (10 oz) fresh cabbage, 1 or 2 carrots, a dint each of salt and sugar, a handful of cranberry, vegetable oil, lettuce leaves

Chop fresh cabbage in narrow strips and grate carrots on a coarse shredder. Salt the cabbage slightly and rub it with your hands so that it becomes juicy. Combine it with the carrots, season with sugar and vegetable oil to taste, put into a salad-bowl over lettuce leaves, and sprinkle with cranberries.

Beetroot Salad with Prunes

2 boiled beetroots, 2/3 cup prunes, 2 cloves garlic, a handful of walnuts, salt, sugar, vegetable oil, lettuce leaves

Grate beetroots on a coarse shredder. Soak prunes in cold boiled water for 4 hours, drain off water, remove pits, cut pulp in strips and add them to the grated beetroots. Add chopped walnuts and garlic. Season with salt, sugar and vegetable oil. Spread the salad over lettuce leaves into a salad-bowl and decorate it with halves of walnut kernels.

Potato Salad, Russian Style

300 g (10 oz) boiled potatoes, 100 g (3½ oz) boiled carrots, 200 g (7 oz) green peas, 100 g (3½ oz) salted mushrooms, 2 salted cucumbers, 1 apple, 1 root of apple celery, salt, vegetable oil

Dice potatoes, carrots, celery and apple, finely mince salted mushrooms, combine all the ingredients, add green peas, season with vegetable oil and, if desired, salt.

Beetroot with Garlic

300 g (10 oz) young beetroot, 2 or 3 cloves garlic, a bunch each of green onions and lettuce, vegetable oil

Peel young beetroots boiled in jackets, cut them into thin rounds, place on a serving dish covered with lettuce leaves, sprinkle with minced garlic and decorate with leaves of green onions. Serve vegetable oil separately.

Young beetroot is tasty with horse-radish too.

Beans with Spices

300 g (10 oz) beans, 1 tsp. sugar, 1 tbsp. dried carrots, 1 tbsp. roots each: celery, parsnip and parsley, 1 or 2 bay leaves, a dint of ground spices: cinnamon, nutmeg, ginger, ground red and black pepper and coriander, salt

Sort out beans, wash and pour over water, add sugar and boil covered until tender. Season with salt and spices and cook until completely ready.

Rice, Monastery Style

1 cup rice, 2 onions, 2 tbsp. vegetable oil, 2 carrots, 1 tbsp. tomato paste, salt, a dint of sugar, ground black and red pepper, dried green dill, lovage and parsnip

Wash rice changing water seven times, pour over boiling water in the proportion of 1 to 2, boil for 10 minutes and strain through a colander. Sauté minced onion with a dint of sugar in a deep pan with heated vegetable oil until golden. Then add to the onion boiled carrots shredded on a coarse grater and tomato paste. Add rice, mix up, heat for 5 to 7 minutes, season with salt, pepper and dried herbs. Serve the dish hot.

Beetroot Salad with Herring

1 herring, 2 or 3 potatoes, 2 carrots, 1 beetroot, 2 salted cucumbers, 1 onion, a bunch of green onions, vegetable oil, ground black pepper

Boil vegetables, cool and cut into dices. Skin herring, bone the fillet and cut it into small pieces. Dice cucumbers, mince green onions and cut an onion bulb into rings. Season beetroot with vegetable oil separately and mix up. Combine all the ingredients. Season the salad with vegetable oil and pepper, without adding salt. Decorate the dish with rings of onion or with a flower made of onion.

Dacha Beetroot Salad

2 potatoes, 2 carrots, 1 beetroot, 100 g (3½ oz) cauliflower, 500 g (1 lb 2 oz) green pies, lettuce leaves, dill and parsley, vegetable oil, salt, ground black pepper, 1 clove garlic or a green leaf of garlic

Boil potatoes, carrots and beetroot, cool and dice them. Boil and cool cauliflower and break it into florets. Combine all the ingredients, add green peas and minced herbs. Add salt, pepper and vegetable oil.

Pie with Salted Mushrooms

For the dough: 6 to 7 cups wheat flour, 50 g (1¾ oz) yeast, 2 cups lukewarm water, ½ cup vegetable oil, salt and sugar
For the filling: 1 to 1.3 kg (2 lb 3 oz to 2 lb 14 oz) salted mushrooms, 5 or 6 onions, vegetable oil, ground black pepper

Knead lenten yeast dough, cover it with a napkin and put in a hot place for fermentation. Prepare mushroom filling. Cut salted mushrooms (if too salted, rinse them with cold water) by a chopper or cut like noodles and sauté in vegetable oil. Sauté shredded onion separately, combine mushrooms and onions and season with pepper. The filling should be piquant.

Roll the dough out into an oblong fitting the size of the baking sheet, place on the baking sheet and prick with a fork. Spread the mushroom filling and cover it by the dough, link and pinch the edges bending the seam of the pie down. Prick the surface of the pie with a fork and brush with a sweet tea. Bake the pie at 356° to 392° F until ready. After baking grease the pie with vegetable oil.

Pie with mushrooms, simple to cook and savoury, is very good for fasting periods. It is served with sour *shchi*, *borshch*, mushroom soup or tea and, on festive occasions, as an appetizer with vodka.

Carrot Salad

4 or 5 carrots, lemon juice, 2 tbsp. chopped walnuts, 10 whole walnut kernels, a dint each of salt and sugar

Grate carrots, season them with salt, sugar and lemon juice, mix with chopped walnuts and decorate with whole walnut kernels.

Pie with Carrots

Yeast dough: 1.2 kg (2 lb 10 oz)
For the filling: 10 medium-sized carrots, lemon juice, 1 or 2 tbsp. vegetable oil, salt and sugar to taste

Roll dough into a round cake about ½-inch thick. Place it on a buttered baking sheet and prick with a fork. Spread grated carrot filling over the dough and bend its edges so that they form a rim ¾-inch wide. The rim can be decorated with leaves and flowers made of dough and greased with a sweet tea. You may also drop several poppy seeds and grated carrots in the middle of the flowers. Bake the pie at 356° to 392° F until ready.

For the filling, pare carrots, shred them on a fine grater, blanch after adding 1 or 2 tablespoons of water, butter, lemon juice, salt and sugar, lowering the heat to the minimum in a covered vessel stirring periodically.

Borshch with Sauerkraut

800 g (1 lb 12 oz) beetroot, 500 g (1 lb 2 oz) sauerkraut, 350 g (12 oz) potatoes, 1 carrot, 1 onion, 2 tbsp. tomato paste, vegetable oil, salt, sugar, parsley root, fresh or dried herbs

Cut beetroot into narrow strips or grind it on a coarse grater and stew adding tomato paste and vegetable oil. Stew sauerkraut with vegetable oil and sugar. Drop sliced potatoes into boiling water and cook for 7 to 10 minutes, then add the sauerkraut, the beetroot (boil for 7 minutes) as well as carrot and parsley root shredded on a coarse grater and slightly browned in butter. Season with green dill, parsley or celery, salt and sugar, remove from heat and let stand for 15 to 20 minutes.

Serve *borshch* with rye bread, herbs, green onions or a bulb of onion.

Fried Jerusalem Artichoke

Peeled tubers of Jerusalem artichokes are very tasty when eaten raw, their flavour being like that of walnuts. The taste of fried artichokes is close to that of potatoes, but tubers of artichoke contain, instead of starch, carbohydrate inulin useful in the treatment of diabetics.

Peel artichoke, cut it in round slices, fry in vegetable oil and salt.

Serve as a garnish with meat or as an independent dish.

Stocked up products are a good help for a housewife, especially when the season of fresh vegetables is over and your table needs a variety. Then comes the time of food-stuffs kept in stock.

FESTIVE RECIPES

*T*here are many church feasts and secular festivals in Russia as elsewhere. The most significant holidays are celebrated all over the vast country. Usually these festivities are accompanied by popular merry-making, traditional games, dances, amusements and other pleasant pastimes.

On festive occasions most of the families lay the table which is marked by abundance, magnificence and a great variety of traditional dishes and articles cooked and served only on these memorable days.

Christmas and New Year Festivities

In 1700 Peter the Great issued a decree that the New Year should begin on 1 January rather than on 1 September as before.

Christmas celebrations naturally merged with those of the New Year and became known as Christmas Tide. Christmas Eve, the evening of 6 January, was remarkable as a day when mummers and carol-singers went from house to house with a "star" (burning candle) performing a play devoted to the Nativity of Christ and singing Christmas carols. They were presented with money, pies, *koliadkas*, honey cakes and gingerbread.

© Н.Орлеанский 1997г.

The Russian name of Christmas Tide, *sochelnik*, originated from the word *sochivo*, a ritual dish to be eaten during this evening. *Sochivo* is made of almond juice, poppy-seed with honey and a cereal of red wheat, barley, rye or millet, which in recent times is usually substituted by rice. During the second day of the Nativity Festival "granny's *kasha*" or *kutya* was eaten. Unlike the Christmas fasting *kutya*, the granny's *kasha* was cooked "rich".

There is hardly any other festival which can rival the days of Christmas and Christmas-Tide (from Christmas to Baptism Day) in merriment and amusements: the decoration of the sparkling New Year Trees, children's holidays with long-awaited gifts, the ritual of young girls' fortune-telling, etc. Christmas merry-making included masquerades, carnivals, songs, dances and merry-go-rounds. Wealthy people organized charity dinners. Christmas Tide was the time to pay visits to relatives and good friends and to receive guests. All these winter festivities took place around the hospitably laid table. According to tradition, it was first sprinkled with hay – as a memory of the Holy Family's cave and manger, then it was covered with a snow-white tablecloth, with *sochivo* as a centrepiece and all dishes, twelve in number, arranged around it: fish courses, fish or meat in aspic, meat jelly, a suckling-pig, a pig head with horse-radish, home-made pork sausage, roast, gingerbread, honey cakes, breadsticks with poppy-seed and honey and stewed fruits.

Stuffed Pike-Perch

For 1 kg (2 lb 3 oz) of fish fillet: 150 g (5 oz) fried onion, 100 g (3½ oz) raw onion, 250 g (8½ oz) white bread without crusts, 3 uncooked eggs, chopped garlic, salt, ground black pepper, a dint of sugar, a walnut-sized piece of butter or 1 tbsp. vegetable oil

Clean and scale fish, remove, through a cut in the back, its spine incised near the head and tail, remove its intestines, cut off its rib bones and nearly the entire meat leaving on the skin only a layer about ¼-inch thick. Put the removed meat through a mincer, add white bread soaked in milk, wrung out and sautéed, and raw onion, chopped garlic, eggs, and butter. Put all this through a mincer again, season with salt, sugar, pepper and minced greens, mix up and stuff the fish with minced meat. Wrap the fish in a gauze, tie up in several places by a cord, put on a grid in a fish cauldron, pour over water, add cucumber brine, salted cucumbers, carrots and celery and simmer covered. At the end of boiling drop spices: bay leaf, black pepper and sweet peas. Time of boiling: 1 hour per 1 kg (2 lb 3½ oz). Cool the ready fish in its concoction, remove the cord and the gauze, lay the pike-perch on a serving dish and make decorations of butter in the cut spots with a bag, place olives into eye-sockets and also adorn them. Garnish with pies, olives and greens.

Sochivo (Christmas Dish)

1 cup wheat grains, 2/3 cup poppy-seed, 2/3 cup walnut kernels, 2 to 3 tablespoons honey, sugar to taste

To make *sochivo*, a Russian Christmas dish, you should prepare wheat grains – crush them in a wooden mortar by a pestle, adding water from time to time, to completely free grains from their hulls. Then separate the cores from weeds by winnowing, sifting and washing the grains. Use the clean grains to boil a usual fasting thin crispy *kasha*. Cool it and sweeten to taste. Honey is preferable as a sweetener, although part of it may be replaced, for economic purposes, with sugar.

Separately, in a special vessel, grind poppy-seed until you receive poppy milk, add honey, mix until well blended, and add to the *kasha*. If the *kasha* is thick, thin it with cooled boiled water. Walnut kernels are added last.

Sochivo may be also cooked of rice. The proportions of its ingredients are the same. Sometimes raisins boiled until tender, are added. The ready dish should be succulent, rice grains should be whole, that is, each particle must be separate.

Meat-Jelly

2 cow feet and lips, 1 carrot, 1 root each of parsley, celery and parsnip, 1 or 2 bay leaves, 10 black peppercorns, salt, garlic

Put meat prepared for the jelly into a large cast-iron vessel or a casserole, add roots, pour cold water and boil first over a high heat skimming off the foam regularly, then simmer covered for no less than 6 hours. When the roots are ready take them out by a straining spoon and continue to boil the jelly until meat separates from bones and the stock acquires a glueing consistency. Add salt and spices some 15 minutes before the end of boiling. Then sift the stock through a napkin, bone meat and cut it into small pieces, put it into moulds, decorate with star-shaped pieces of carrot and other roots, if desired, add minced garlic, pour in sifted stock, let it chill in a cold larder or refrigerator (put the cooled jelly into a refrigerator covered).

Meat jelly is a popular Russian cold appetizer. It is commonly seasoned with horse-radish, mustard, mayonnaise and vinegar, and served at a festive table with vodka.

Goose Stuffed with Apples

1 goose, 10 to 15 cooking apples, a handful of raisins, 1 tsp. caraway seed, 1 tsp. marjoram, salt, green parsley and celery, soaked paradise apples, red whortleberries or red whortleberry jam

Rub the body and cavity with salt and chopped caraway and marjoram. Peel, core and half apples. Mix them with washed and soaked raisins. Stuff the bird with the halves of apples and sew the goose up. Sprinkle the bottom of a pan with dry wine, lay the bird on the pan with its back down, having it brushed with cream or fat, and place it into a well heated oven. If the bird is not sufficiently plump, to make it brown well, baste it with honey mixed with wine, sour cream and drippings and pour it with pomegranate juice. Turn over the bird from time to time. When the goose becomes brown, you may test its readiness with the help of a needle pricking the bird in several places. Light gravy is a reliable evidence that the goose is ready. Discard the thread, remove the apples and raisins, cut the bird into portions, arrange them on a serving dish to imitate an uncut goose and put on curling-papers. Place around the bird the cooking apples, soaked cranberries, small paradise apples and green parsley.

Baked Mutton Leg

Put a mutton leg into salted water, add vinegar and keep for 8 hours. Then cut off films from the surface of the meat and lard it with mutton fat and garlic. Perform this operation in the following way: make a deep slash in the meat by the sharp edge of a knife, push a piece of mutton fat into it and then drive in the sharp end of a clove of garlic like a nail. Rub the mutton leg above with salt, without pepper, lay it on a buttered baking sheet and bake in the oven at 410° F. 40 minutes later turn the ham over and continue to bake on the other side for about the same time. Place peeled and halved potatoes around the mutton and bake them together with it until ready.

Baked Salted Pork

Loin of pork, salt, nutmeg, garlic

Rub a ham or the loin of pork and bake in the oven with a small layer of fat and a mixture of garlic, nutmeg and salt until golden, then reduce heat and bring the pork to full readiness often pouring it with drippings. The time of cooking: 1.5 to 2.5 hours, depending on the size of the ham or loin of pork. Test readiness by pricking the meat with a needle. If the dripping is transparent, the dish is ready.

Home-Made Pork Sausage

1 kg (2 lb 3 oz) pork, 2 or 3 onions, 1 or 2 cloves garlic, salt, ground black pepper, bay leaf, nutmeg, marjoram

Put pork with onions through a mincer, or better chop it by a knife – in this case sausage will be

more tasty. Season the minced meat with salt, pepper, nutmeg, bay leaf, dried marjoram, mix up, use the pork to fill accordingly prepared pig's intestines and tie the ends with a thread. Lay the filled sausage into a pan as a ring or spiral, sprinkle the pan with some dry wine, prick the sausage with a needle to let out air which has penetrated inside when filling the sausage. Bake the sausage in the oven on both sides often pouring it with drippings. Serve the browned fragrant home-made sausage at the festive table hot with boiled or fried potatoes, fresh greens, soaked red whortleberry and other delicious home-made things. Serve wholesome, noble beverages to drink with them.

Honey Cakes: *Festive Present*

For the dough: 2½ cups flour, 300 g (10 oz) honey, 1 egg, 1/3 cup sour cream, ¼ cup butter, 1 tsp. mixture
of cinnamon, cardamom and anise, 0.5 tsp. soda and lemon juice, a dint of salt
For the greasing: 1 egg
For the decoration: white, pink and chocolate glazing, nonpareil, streusel, nuts

Heat honey by the water-bath method until warm and mix it with butter, sour cream, egg, ground cinnamon, cardamom and anise, as well as with soda, lemon juice and salt. Stir the mixture well, add sifted flour and knead dough. Let it rest for 2 or 3 hours and then roll into a piece ¼ to ½-inch thick and, for the largest tins, to 1/3-inch thick. Cut out "hearts" of various dimensions with the help of moulds, grease them with egg, bake on buttered metal sheets at 392° F and chill. Glaze the cakes and paint them over with sugar, cranberry or chocolate glazing and pass varicoloured bands through them.

Honey Cakes: *Honey Heart*

2½ cups wheat flour, 300 g (10 oz) honey, ¾ cup confectioners' sugar, ¼ cup butter, 2 eggs, ½ tsp. soda, lemon juice, ½ tsp. chopped
cinnamon, anise and cardamom

Heat honey by the water-bath method until warm and mix it with butter. Mix up confectioners' sugar with eggs, cinnamon, anise, cardamom, soda, and lemon juice. Mix the dough with flour and let it stay for 5 hours. Then roll the dough to ¾" thickness, cut it into heart shapes with the aid of a special mould, brush them lightly with egg, lay on a pan greased with butter, bake, glaze with coloured icings, sprinkle with chopped nuts and almonds and coloured strands (streusel and nonpareil) and decorate with painted design.

Honey Cake: Petrushka

For the dough: 2¼ cups rye flour, ½ cup butter, 250 g (8½ oz) honey, 1 egg, 2 tbsp. cranberry ground with sugar, 1 tsp. soda, a dint of salt
For the glazing: 1 egg white, ¾ cup confectioners' sugar, lemon juice
For the decoration: raisins, walnut kernels, almond kernels in petals, ground coconut, nonpareil, streusel, crushed nuts

    Melt butter, mix with honey, egg, cranberry rubbed with sugar, soda and salt. Mix all until well blended, add flour, knead dough and let it stay for 2 hours. Roll the dough ¼ to ½-inch thick and, using the dough and a mould, cut out the figurines of a clown, bake them, cool and decorate with glazing. Such bright toy gingerbread is a highly desirable gift for children.

Boris Kustodiev. *Shrovetide. 1916. The Russian Museum, St Petersburg*

*S*hrovetide

A long time before sour bread had been developed, many peoples celebrated holidays when, according to tradition, unleavened bread was baked and presented to relatives and good friends. There is an opinion that baking bread or pancakes, *oladyi* in Russian, has been connected with the arrival of the spring and the coming of spring birds, larks (or *olaudae*)., Ethnologists and folklore specialists assert that Shrovetide rituals are exclusively heathen ones. In the old times, there was a custom to commemorate ancestors by pancakes during the Paternal Week, on the eve of Shrovetide. The seeing-off of the receding winter and the meeting of the long-awaited spring, the arrival of larks, its first harbingers, all this is widely reflected in the Shrovetide merry-making celebrated on a large scale. Shrovetide, as the last week before Lent, is a cheese week, when meat is not allowed any more, but one can eat cheese, butter, eggs, sour cream, cottage cheese, fritters, pancakes and pies. The tradition has survived to the present day – the merry festival is celebrated by nearly everybody in Russia. Once Shrovetide merry-making used to last for the whole week and included such merry pastimes as driving ornate carriages and riding horses, the taking of a snow fortress and the building of ice houses, fisticuffs or visits to relatives and friends. Each day had its own title: Monday was "meeting", Tuesday meant "entertainment", Wednesday implied "dainties", Thursday" was known as "Wide Thursday", Friday was associated with "the mother-in-law's evening parties", Saturday was "sisters-in-law's gatherings" and Sunday was called "seeing-off, or Absolution Sunday". Many merry jokes, songs, proverbs and sayings are connected with these festive days. A lot of them are devoted to festive meals and favourite dishes.

Pancakes and *blinis* are in particular favour with the Russians – they are a good hot *zakuska* for vodka and an indispensable accompaniment to tea or coffee. The Russian cuisine possesses a vast repertory of fillings for pancakes: minced meat with onions, chicken meat, cottage cheese, jam, fresh berries, garden and wild berries and mushrooms. *Blinis* are used as delicious wrappers for salted fish as well as for salmon and sturgeon caviar.

Instant Russian Blinis

5 tbsp. flour, 2½ cups milk, 2 eggs, 1 tbsp. sugar, 1/3 tsp. salt,
2 to 3 tbsp. vegetable oil

Beat eggs, salt and sugar, pour in milk, add flour and mix. Add vegetable oil, stir again and began to bake *blinis* on a preheated pan. Grease the pan with butter before baking the first thin pancake.

Serve instant *blinis* hot with red or black caviar or salmon, with butter, sour cream, jam for tea or coffee or as an appetizer for vodka.

Pie with Dried Apricots in Sour Cream Sauce

Yeast dough: 1 kg (2 lb 3 oz)
For the filling: 600 to 700 g (1 lb 5 oz to 1 lb 9 oz) of choice dried apricots, 3 tbsp. sugar
For the sauce: ¾ cup sour cream, 2 eggs, 1 tsp. sugar
For the greasing: 1 egg yolk

Roll dough into a layer ¼-inch thick and place it into a buttered round mould or pan so that it overlaps the edges of the mould. Blanch dried apricots in a small quantity of water adding sugar, and strain the syrup. Cool the dried apricots, spread on the dough and pour over sour cream whipped with eggs and sugar, fold up the edge of the pie, decorate it with leaves made of dough and brush with egg yolk. Bake at 356° to 392° F until brown.

Festive Breadsticks

For the dough: 4 cups wheat flour, 7 eggs, 2 tbsp. confectioners' sugar, ¼ cup butter, a wineglass vodka or cognac, a dint of salt
For the frying: olive oil

Beat eggs with salt and sugar, mix with butter, vodka or cognac, and pour the mixture gradually into a depression made in a mound of sifted flour (the flour must be dry). Knead thick pliable dough, cover it with a napkin and leave for 20 minutes to rest. Then shape it as camomiles, chrysanthemums and rosettes.

For camomiles, cut out of thinly rolled dough (½-inch thick), using cutters, pieces of various diameter shaped as flowers. Outline and shape their petals, put into boiling fat and fry on both sides until golden, take out of the boiling fat by a perforated spoon and chill. The daffodil will look more inviting if before deep-fat frying you have combined three flowers: the smallest above, and the largest below, glueing them in the centre by an egg.

For the chrysanthemums, cut the thinly rolled dough into rectangles about 1½ by 2½ inches. Slightly incise the longer end of each piece into narrow strips ½ to ¾-inch wide and 1¼-inch long and roll the partly cut end into a tube, prick it on a fork and dip its freely hanging petals into the boiling fat keeping the piece on the fork until the petals unfold and harden. After that the entire piece can be immersed for frying.

To make a rosette, use a sharp knife to cut out of the thinly rolled dough pieces reminiscent of an open parachute. Firmly link the opposite ends of each piece and insert them one into the other so that each subsequent one would overlap the preceding piece forming a bud or rose. It is sufficient to make 3 petals for a bud, and 5 to 7 ones for a rose.

Arrange the ready breadsticks attractively in a basket or on a serving dish and serve at the table.

Leaf-Shaped Blinis

Prepare dough in the same way as indicated in the recipe for Instant Russian Blinis.
For the filling: 1¼ cups fresh cottage cheese, 2 tbsp. sugar, 2 tbsp. sour cream, 2 egg yolks or 1 egg, salt to taste
For the frying: ½ cup butter

Leaf-shaped *blinis* differ from their common instant variety by their shape. To prepare leaf-shaped *blinis*, put a filling on each piece, roll it into a cigarette-like tube and bake in butter on a pan.

The festive version of the leaf-shaped *blinis* is somewhat more complex. Tie up a pancake rolled as a cigarette with a thread, grease it with egg, roll in bread crumbs and bake in boiling oil. Discard the thread before serving.

"Red" or Fine Blinis

For the leaven: 2½ cup flour, 25 g (¾ oz) yeast, 2 cups baked milk
For the dough: 5 egg yolks, 2/3 cups butter, 2½ cups flour, salt and sugar to taste, 5 egg whites

Use flour, warm milk and yeast to prepare leaven and let it stand in a warm place for 1 or 1.5 hours. When the leaven rises, add butter rubbed with egg yolks, sugar and salt until white, sift flour and knead smooth dough. Put in a warm place. When the dough rises for the second time, add egg whites beaten up until frothy, stir carefully from top to bottom and after 10 to 15 minutes began to bake *blinis*.

A custom to invite gypsies during holidays was widely popular in Russian society. Even nowadays, a banquet is often inconceivable without their merry chorus and fiery dances.

Easter is the most favourite and merry spring festival celebrated by the Russians with reverence, sweep and joy. It is no surprise that formerly it was accompanied by a number of beautiful customs whose origins go deep back into history. Each housewife began to prepare for Easter with the arrival of the Great Week, the last week of the Lenten Fast. Starting on Great Thursday, each family was preparing for a festive table: painted eggs, cooked the *Paskha*, baked the Easter Cake, pies, *blinis*, small pasties shaped as rams, cockerels, hens, doves and larks, as well as honey cakes and gingerbread. Easter dishes were never repeated within a year, except for painted eggs (for Trinity Day, though, they were painted green).

Much food was cooked for the Easter table: a lamb and veal were baked, hams were smoked. Hot dishes were not available at the Easter table and it was also a custom not to serve fish on that day. The table was marked by a festive magnificence – it was tasty, lavish and beautiful. The Easter Cake and the *Paskha* were usually embellished with flowers. The making of flowers for the holiday used to be a very entertaining occupation, as was naturally the painting of eggs.

honey cakes. The festival lasted throughout the Holy Week and the table remained laid to treat to anybody who happened to come. In the evening, with the arrival of dusk, there was a tradition to play violin in villages. Violinists wandered from one village to another and played under the windows of each house celebrating the Resurrection of Christ and the residents would treat them to a glass of wine and present with Easter eggs and sometimes money.

According to ancient tradition, painted eggs were put on a fresh outgrowth of barley, wheat or on soft green tiny leaves of cress which were specially grown indoors for the festival.

Easter was considered to be a family festival. Children were presented with real painted eggs and their chocolate imitations and with

Smoked Ham, Village Style

The preparation of this culinary masterpiece combines consequentially several processes: salting, dry-curing and smoking. Pork ham is usually lavishly sprinkled with salt or wholly dipped in brine (2.5 pounds salt per 2.2 gal.) bucket. The brine should be sifted and cooled. Add to the solution bay leaf, black peppercorns, caraway seed and several cloves of garlic. Hams need no less 7 to 10 days of soaking in the brine. Salted hams are kept in wooden barrels or boxes in a cold storeroom until February or early March.

Hung hams for dry-curing in a well-ventilated room – it is important that it is accessible for sunlight. Towards evening the hams are removed to a dark cool ventilated room. The ultra-violet rays promote the formation of a crust on the surface of the ham and therefore are good for the quality of the meat and render it a peculiar taste and flavour.

Ham is especially tasty when smoked. As a rule smoking of hams is performed in April or early May, on the eve of Easter. A special oven and materials necessary for smoking are prepared: green fir twigs giving dense white smoke, alder sawdust and chips.

For a more subtle flavour twigs of various fruit trees are used: apple-trees, cherries, plum-trees, bushes of currants, as well as juniper needles which, moreover, have an antiseptic action. The simplest room used for smoking in a village usually is a bath-house.

Hung dried hams from the ceiling using cross bars or hooks. Dismantle the flooring and lit a fire on the ground. Smoke hams on white cold smoke for 4 to 7 days with closely shut doors and windows (without flame!) at an average room temperature. Make sure that smoke evenly envelops the hams. During the first two days ventilate the room for 3 to 4 hours. During the last day temperature in the room should be raised to 95–98° F and maintained for a day. Strictly observe the indicated temperature scheme and the process of smoking for a week throughout day and night time.

This method is, as it were, a combination of dry and hot smoking variants. Smoked ham is an exqui-site delicacy on a festive table. It is served with an abundance of piquant greens, fresh vegetables and salads, either pure, without any additions, or with soaked red whortleberry, paradise apples, salted or fresh cucumbers and drinks, which are matching this culinary masterpiece.

Baked Suckling-Pig

Put a singed, disembowelled and cleaned suckling pig for 4 to 8 hours into a marinade – cooled boiled water with an addition of lemon juice, bay leaf and black peppercorns. After pickling, clean the body until white, dry it with a napkin, salt inside and out, grease with softened butter and put into a 428° F oven. When the pig is brown, reduce the heat to 302 or

320° F. To prevent burning of the most vulnerable place – the ears of the pig, we recommend you to put egg shells on them or plaster them by the dough of flour, water and salt. Determine the readiness of the dish by means of a needle pricking the pig in the neck area. If transparent drippings appear, the pig is ready.

Suckling pig is a festive dish served to the table on Christmas, Easter and to mark a wedding ceremony or other similar ceremonial occasions.

Orthodox Easter Cake

6 cups wheat flour, ½ cup milk, 50 to 70 g (1½ to 2½ oz) fresh yeast, 1 cup sugar, 5 eggs, 1¼ cup butter, 200 g (7 oz) almond kernels, 1 lemon, 150 g (5 oz) raisins, salt to taste

Boil the milk and cool it to the temperature of that fresh from the cow. Use a small part of the milk to dissolve the yeast, add 1 tablespoon sugar. Put sifted flour in the milk, add foaming yeast, mix thoroughly and, covering by a towel, let it stay in a warm place for fermentation. When the dough raises, add 5 beaten egg yolks, warm (not hot) melted butter, ground lemon rind, part of unshelled almond kernels, raisins,

tractively glazed. For this, whip 1 egg white with ¾ to 1 cup of confectioners' sugar. The sugar should be of the finest grinding and sifted through a fine sieve. Add the sugar gradually, one teaspoon at a time, and whip the egg white without interrupting (better by hands rather than by a mixer). The ready glazing should be sticky, but a little fluid and at the same time fluffy; it should not be too diffuse. Glazing may be tinted with cranberry or lemon juice. All decorations (nonpareil, nuts, raisins and dried apricots) are to be spread over yet unhardened glazing.

Easter Cake

For the dough: 350 g (12 oz) butter, 1½ cups sugar, 300 g (10 oz) cottage cheese, 5 egg yolks, 2 egg whites, 2 tbsp. honey, 1 handful each of almond and walnut kernels and raisins, 1 tbsp. candied orange peel, 1 tsp. ground lemon with peel, 1 tsp. soda, a dint each of salt and vanilla, 3 cups flour
For the glazing: 1 egg white, 2/3 to ¾ cup confectioners' sugar, 2 tbsp. ground cranberry
For the decoration: nonpareil

Rub butter with half of sugar, add sieved cottage cheese, egg yolks beaten with the rest of the sugar, honey, minced almond and walnut kernels, candied orange peels, raisins, ground lemon, soda, salt and vanilla. Mix all the ingredients, pour sifted flour, quickly knead dough and put it into a buttered cake tin with a pipe. Bake at 356° to 392° F for one hour. Glaze the cooled cake and sprinkle it with nonpareil.

salt, egg whites beaten until frothy with the second part of the sugar. Carefully knead the dough stirring it from top to bottom so that to preserve the structure of the foam as much as possible. If required, during kneading flour may be added, but before introducing beaten egg whites – this condition is obligatory to be fulfilled. Place the dough into special Easter Cake moulds greased with softened butter, allow the dough rise level with the edges of the mould, brush over the top of the cake with the beaten yolk of egg, sprinkle with almond kernels and bake until ready at 356° to 392° F. Do not hurry to take baked cakes from the moulds – they can break, sink, harden, lose shape or appearance. The cakes must get cool. The chilled cake can be at-

Royal Paskha (Sweet Easter Dish)

2 cups butter, 5 or 6 egg yolks, 2 cups sugar, 4 cups cottage cheese, 1¼ cups 30% cream, 100 g (3½ oz) each raisins, almonds and candied peels, cardamom or vanilla

Rub butter with sugar until white gradually adding egg yolks one at a time. Rub paste until sugar completely dissolves, add vanilla or minced and sifted through a fine sieve cardamom for flavour. Add cottage cheese twice grated on a fine shredder, raisins, almonds, candied orange peels or grated lemon rinds. Mix thoroughly, add whipped cream and stir from top to bottom. Fill the paste into a special *paskha* mould over a slightly wet gauze, cover it with a saucer, press by a small weight and refrigerate for 12 hours.

Royal Blinis

For the leaven: 3 cups wheat flour, 50 g (1½ oz) yeast, ½ cup or a little more milk
For the dough: 6 egg yolks, ¾ cup butter, salt and sugar to taste, 3 cups flour, 1¼ cups 30% cream, 6 egg whites

Prepare leaven from the warmed milk, yeast and flour. When it rises, add egg yolks ground with butter, salt and sugar until well blended. Sift flour through a sieve, mix the dough thoroughly, put into a warm place for fermentation from 40 to 60 minutes. When the dough rises again, add separately cream and egg whites beaten until frothy, stir the dough from top to bottom and begin to bake *blinis*.

Best served with caviar and salmon.

Honey Cake: Cockerel and Hen Figurines

For the dough: 2½ wheat flour, 350 g (12 oz) honey, ¼ cup butter, 2 egg whites, 1 tsp. mixture of ground spices, a dint of soda, 1 tsp. lemon juice, a dint of salt
For the greasing: 2 egg yolks
For the glazing; 1 egg white, 2/3 to ¾ cup confectioners' sugar, cranberry juice
For the dressing: nonpareil, coloured streusel, minced almonds and walnuts, coconut chips

Melt butter, combine with honey, spices, soda, lemon juice and salt, mix until well blended. Add sifted flour and egg whites beaten until frothy, knead a dough. Roll it into a layer ½ or ¾-inch thick, cut out of the dough cockerels and hens in special moulds, brush them with egg yolk and bake on buttered baking sheets at 356° to 392° F until brown.

Cool the cockerel and hen figurines, paint them and glaze with white sugar and pink cranberry glazing. After glazing sprinkle the honey cakes with minced nuts, nonpareil, and streusel. The honey cakes can be painted after baking and cooling, before or after glazing and complete chilling of the surface.

INDEX

Text by Lydia Liakhovskaya
Translated from the Russian by Valery Fateyev
Designed by Nikolai Kutovoi
Illustrations by Anton Lomayev and Alexei Orleansky
Computer type-setting by Yelena Morozova and Alexander Shcheglov
Colour proofs by Liubov Kornilova and Vladimir Glazkov
Photographs by Georgy Khordas, Arthur Kirakozov, Lydia Liakhovskaya,
Vladimir Melnikov, Victor Poliakov, Yekaterina Posetselskaya, Victor Savik,
Vladimir Vdovin, Vasily Vorontsov and Victor Yeremeyev
Editor-in-Chief: Sergei Vesnin
Managing editor: Maria Lyzhenkova

The publishers are thankful to Sergei E. Gutzeit, the owner of the Podvoriye Restaurant,
for a great help and support in the preparation of this art book.